Honoring Your Heritage of Faith

Why God Wants You To Develop and Perpetuate a Life of Faith

by
Jerry Savelle

Harrison House
Tulsa, Oklahoma

Honoring Your Heritage of Faith — Why God Wants You To Develop and Perpetuate a Life of Faith
ISBN 0-89274-732-3
Copyright © by Jerry Savelle
P. O. Box 748
Crowley, Texas 76036

Published by Harrison House, Inc.
P. O. Box 35035
Tulsa, Oklahoma 74153

Contents

Contents

Introduction

Some time ago the Spirit of the Lord impressed a message upon my heart which I shared in a Believers' Convention in Australia. Since that time He has expanded and expounded upon that basic message, adding new insight into some things from His Word that we have all embraced and held dear for a number of years now.

That vital message from the Spirit and Word of the Lord has been growing bigger and bigger on the inside of me, and I have been tremendously blessed by it. I believe you will be too. I have been preaching it everywhere I go and have put together a series of cassette tapes on it. It has become a revelation to many hundreds of people. I believe that if you will allow it to do so, it will minister to you just as it has to all these others. It will cause an understanding of the life of faith to drop down into your spirit that you have never known before in your entire life.

The Word of God is so exciting and so inexhaustible. Just about the time we think we have learned all there is to know about a certain verse or passage of Scripture, the Lord will show us that there is much more revelation knowledge to be gained from it.

In Isaiah 33:6 we are told, **...wisdom and knowledge shall be the stability of thy times....** If there is one thing the Body of Christ needs today, it is stability. We are living in a very shaky world and in very unsettled times. I don't know about you, but I would hate to think that I had to live in this day and hour without the Word of God. I would hate to think that I was without Christ, without the ability to tap into a higher knowledge than that offered by the world in which we live. Thank God that we have access to wisdom that comes from above. With that revelation knowledge and that divine wisdom, we can find stability in a very unstable environment.

"The Faith Message Is Over"?

...the just shall *live* by faith....

Hebrews 10:38

One of the reasons the Spirit of the Lord kept dealing with me to study and speak about the subject I am sharing with you in these pages is because of the wrong attitude that has seemed to develop in recent years. I kept hearing people, even preachers, say that the faith message is no longer needed.

One minister even had the audacity to tell me to my face, "That message that you and Kenneth Copeland and Kenneth Hagin and people like you preach was good for the sixties and the seventies and even the eighties, but it is not the message of the nineties."

That is the most foolish thing I have ever heard in my life!

In this study we are going to be answering some vital questions about the subject of faith as we look at what God has to say about it in His Word.

I believe that if you will follow this message closely with an open heart and mind, the Spirit of the Lord will build up such an immune system within you that when you hear people say such ridiculous things, you will be all the more determined to do as God says and continue to live by faith — regardless of what others may say or do.

When faith has healed your body, your mind, your marriage, your family and your finances, when it has provided you a place to live and clothes to wear and a car to drive and food to eat, then it will be too late for anyone to try to convince you that it is not necessary to live by and pass on your glorious heritage of faith!

1

Unwavering, Uncompromising Faith

And he spake a parable unto them to this end, *that men ought always to pray, and not to faint;*

Saying, There was in a city a judge, which feared not God, neither regarded man:

And there was a widow in that city; and she came unto him, saying, Avenge me of mine adversary.

And he would not for a while: but afterward he said within himself, Though I fear not God, nor regard man;

Yet because this widow troubleth me, I will avenge her, lest by her continual coming she weary me.

Luke 18:1-5

Notice verse 1 which says **...that men ought always to pray, and not to faint.** *The Amplified Bible* translation says **...that they ought always to pray and not to turn coward (faint, lose heart, and give up).** I don't know how it is in your prayer life, but not everything I have ever prayed has manifested instantly. I live continually between "amen" and "there it is."

I thank God for those times when the answer to my prayers is manifested immediately. But that does not happen very frequently. Much more often I have to do what Paul said and **...having done all, to stand. Stand therefore...**(Eph. 6:13,14). Paul also said, **...let us not be**

weary in well doing: for in due season we shall reap, if we faint not (Gal. 6:9).

If you and I exercise faith long enough and "faint not," then sooner or later "due season" always comes!

To illustrate this point, Jesus gives the example of the widow who approached an unjust judge asking him for a ruling against her adversary. Instead, he slammed the door in her face (AP). So she knocked again. When he opened the door, once more she asked the same thing, "Avenge me," and once more she was told, "No!" But she was determined and would not take no for an answer. She kept coming to the judge again and again until finally he decided to give her what she was asking for — not because he really wanted to, but just to keep her from wearing him out with her incessant demands.

What the Lord is illustrating here is not just persistence or determination but unwavering, uncompromising *faith*.

He is saying that this is the way that you and I are to react to the obstacles and hindrances that we face in our lives. Every time the devil slams the door in our face, we are to come right back at him, absolutely determined that we will not accept defeat.

Shall He Find Faith?

And the Lord said, Hear what the unjust judge saith.

And shall not God avenge his own elect, which cry day and night unto him, though he bear long with them?

I tell you that he will avenge them speedily. Nevertheless *when the Son of man cometh, shall he find faith on the earth?*

Luke 18:6-8

Jesus concluded His story by saying, "Listen to what the unjust judge said. If this dishonest man finally avenged this poor woman who kept coming to him, don't you think God will avenge His own elect who cry out to Him day and night? I tell you He will be quick to avenge them."

But then notice His next statement: "Nevertheless when the Son of Man comes back, will He find faith on the earth?"

Obviously, Jesus is going to be looking for something when He returns. What is it? He didn't say, "When the Son of Man returns to the earth, will He find love?" Neither did He say, "When the Son of Man returns to the earth, will He find peace?" Nor did He say, "When the Son of Man returns to the earth, will He find unity?" Instead, He said, "When the Son of Man returns to the earth, will He find faith?" And the reason He said *faith* is because it takes faith to have love and peace and unity.

Evidently the kind of faith that our Lord is going to be looking for when He returns in triumph is that unwavering, uncompromising faith that will not accept defeat. Why? Because He knows that faith is the spiritual force that sustains life.

You and I are not to live by faith simply so we can be contrary to other people. We are not to live by faith just because it sounds like a wonderful idea. We are not to live by faith merely because some preacher said we ought to, although that is very good advice and counsel. We are to live by faith because the Word of God commands us to live that way.

When Jesus returns to this earth, He is not coming for those who have performed some great *act of faith,* but rather for those who have followed a consistent *lifestyle of faith.*

The Three Positions of Faith

...The word is nigh thee, even in thy mouth, and in thy heart: that is, the *word of faith,* which we preach.

Romans 10:8

Where is boasting then? It is excluded. By what law? of works? Nay: but by the *law of faith.*

Romans 3:27

We having the same *spirit of faith,* according as it is written, I believed, and therefore have I spoken; we also believe, and therefore speak.

2 Corinthians 4:13

In these passages from the Apostle Paul we see that there are three positions of faith: 1) the word of faith, 2) the law of faith, and 3) the spirit of faith.

The word of faith is the message. The law of faith is the application or the appropriation of the word of faith. The spirit of faith is the lifestyle of faith.

Let me illustrate this last point about the spirit of faith that we as believers are to manifest twenty-four hours a day.

When our two daughters were young, the older one hated school. She only went because she was obligated to go. Each morning she would drag herself out of bed and put off getting dressed and leaving as long as she possibly could. At school, she would just go through the motions, doing only what she was absolutely required to do, not getting involved in any extracurricular activities she didn't have to and showing little interest in anything that went on. As soon as the last bell rang, she was out of the building like a shot. She hurried home and threw her books on the table where they stayed, unopened if possible, until it was time for her to pick them up and force herself to go back to class. Fortunately, she was smart enough to make great grades, but she always waited until the very last minute to study and prepare herself for exams. In everything related to school, she did only what she had to do — and no more.

The younger daughter was just the opposite. She loved school. Every night she would lay out her clothes in preparation for the coming day. She went to bed each evening thinking about what she would do tomorrow. In the morning she could hardly wait to get out of bed, get dressed, eat breakfast and rush off to meet her friends at school. There she was involved in every kind of activity imaginable. She was in everything. She was a cheerleader, homecoming queen and Miss Crowley High School. She won awards for her studies and received recognition for her extracurricular activities. She not only *loved* to go to school, she *lived* to go to school.

What was the difference between the two girls? They both went to the same school and took the same classes and took part in many of the same functions, but one had spirit, the other didn't. We often speak of "school spirit." My younger daughter had plenty of that! She was so filled with it that everything in her bedroom had to be done in the school colors of purple and white. She didn't go to school because she was obligated to do so, but because she wanted to do so. She was not bound by the law, but led by the Spirit.

The difference that distinguished our two daughters is the same difference that distinguishes many Christians. Some live by the *law of faith*, while others live by the *spirit of faith*. That difference is vitally important.

Faith As a Lifestyle

For therein is the righteousness of God revealed from faith to faith: as it is written, *The just shall live by faith.*

Romans 1:17

Faith is not an act, it is a lifestyle.

Many of us who preach faith are not doing so because we have to. We don't live the way we do because we are required to live that way or because we are afraid not to. We live this way because we have within us the abiding spirit of faith.

Many church members are the same way. When volunteers are called for, four or five of them will jump up and say, "I'll do it, I'll do it!" They are eager to be of service to the Lord and His people.

On the other hand, there are others who come to church out of a sense of obligation. These are the ones who sleep through every service and duck every responsibility.

What is the difference?

Spirit!

Spirit is lifestyle. You can have the word of faith, which is the message, and you may even apply or appropriate it from time to time out of desperation. But when you have the spirit of faith, you don't wake up in the morning wondering whether you should live by faith or not. You don't ask yourself, "Should I continue to stand in faith or should I give up and try something else?" You don't look for options. As far as you're concerned, there are no options, no alternatives. Whatever may lay in store, you step forth in confidence and joy knowing that you are committed heart and soul to the *adventure of faith*!

Jesus said that when He returns to this earth, He will be looking for faith. Our Lord is going to be looking for those people who *live* by faith. Jesus is not going to be looking for people who tried it until the going got rough and then gave up. He is going to be looking for those who have committed themselves to following a consistent *lifestyle* of faith, those who have refused to draw back.

Living by Faith
Versus Drawing Back

Cast not away therefore your confidence, which hath great recompence of reward.

For ye have need of patience, that, after ye have done the will of God, ye might receive the promise.

For yet a little while, and he that shall come will come, and will not tarry.

Now the just shall live by faith: *but if any man draw back, my soul shall have no pleasure in him.*

But we are not of them who draw back unto perdition; but of them that believe to the saving of the soul.

Hebrews 10:35-39

In the first part of verse 38 we see repeated the biblical injunction we read earlier in Romans 1:17: **the**

15

just shall live by faith. This is not an option or a suggestion, it is a command, one that goes all the way back to the Old Testament where we see these same words recorded in Habakkuk 2:4. In the New Testament, this same commandment is repeated in Galatians 3:11. Throughout the Bible, the Lord makes it abundantly clear that He expects those who are righteous to manifest that righteousness by following a consistent lifestyle of faith.

Now notice in the second part of that same verse the Lord's attitude toward anyone who draws back from this consistent lifestyle: **my soul shall have no pleasure in him.**

God has no pleasure in those who cave in, compromise and draw back from the life of faith. That doesn't mean that He doesn't love them, only that He is not pleased with them.

Then in verse 39 the writer of the book of Hebrews goes on to make it clear where he personally stands on this issue: **But we are not of them who draw back unto perdition; but of them that believe to the saving of the soul.**

In other words, he is saying, "I want it made known to everyone that I am not one of those who give up and draw back; rather, I am one of those who believe to the end."

The decision to live by faith or to draw back is one that each of us must make at one time or another in our Christian walk. In this sense, there are only two camps of believers: those who live by faith, and those who try it and end up drawing back.

Don't wait until you are in a storm to decide which group you're going to be a part of. Do it now. Do it the moment that you come into an understanding of the vital concept of living by faith. Make a decision right now that the life of faith is not going to be an experiment with you, but rather a lifestyle. Make up your mind once and for all that this is the way you're going to live from now on.

I must warn you that once you have made that decision, you are going to have many opportunities to draw back. That's when you must draw the line and refuse to step back because you know that God takes no pleasure in those who do.

Why is it so important that you and I live by faith? Why does God insist on this commitment so much? Why is He so inflexible on this point? God is not trying to be cold or harsh. He is not trying to be cruel or unfair. He is not trying to place unnecessary burdens or unreasonable demands upon us.

The reason God requires that we live by faith and not draw back from it is simple: *He is smarter than we are!* The Lord requires us to live by faith because He knows that is the best way to live. He knows that is the way we will derive the most from life. But it goes even deeper than that.

To get at the heart of this matter, let's take a sort of spiritual refresher course. Let's go back to the beginning in the book of Genesis and study the Scriptures to see if we can discover the full reason that God requires that His children live by faith and why He takes no pleasure in those who draw back from the lifestyle of unwavering, uncompromising faith.

2

A Lineage of Faith

And God said, Let us make man in our image, after
our likeness: and let them have dominion over the fish of
the sea, and over the fowl of the air, and over the cattle,
and over all the earth, and over every creeping thing that
creepeth upon the earth.

So God created man in his own image, in the image
of God created he him; male and female created he them.

And God blessed them, and God said unto them, *Be
fruitful, and multiply*, and replenish the earth, and
subdue it: and have dominion over the fish of the sea,
and over the fowl of the air, and over every living thing
that moveth upon the earth.

Genesis 1:26-28

Do you believe that God has faith? Now some
people will answer, "No, because since He's God, He
doesn't need faith."

Personally, I believe with all my heart that God is a
faith Being, that He *lives* by faith. God *operates* by faith
because He calls things not as they are, but as He
envisions them to be. (Rom. 4:17.)

Do you realize what God sees when He looks at His
Church, the Body of Christ? He sees a glorious Church,
one without spot, or wrinkle, or any such thing, one that
is holy and without blemish. (Eph. 5:27.) Why does He
see you and me that way? Because He looks at us from a

spiritual perspective. He sees us not as we are in our natural selves, but as we appear through the blood of His Son Jesus Christ.

And that is faith.

We in the Church have experienced a great deal of shame and reproach lately. The Church has lost more credibility in the past few years than at any other period in our lifetime. Yet God keeps the faith. He keeps right on believing that He has a glorious Church, one without spot or wrinkle or blemish of any kind. And He goes on believing that we are that glorious Church that is going to usher in the return of His Son Jesus Christ to this earth.

That's faith!

Another reason I know that God lives by faith is because I know He *demonstrates* His faith. God *believes* that what He says will come to pass: **So shall my word be that goeth forth out of my mouth: it shall not return unto me void, but it shall accomplish that which I please, and it shall prosper in the thing whereto I sent it** (Is. 55:11). His words carry such creative power that all He has to do is say "Let there be..." and the outcome is "And there it is!"

Creatures of Faith

And Jesus answering saith unto them, *Have faith in God.*

For verily I say unto you, That whosoever shall say unto this mountain, Be thou removed, and be thou cast into the sea; and shall not doubt in his heart, but shall believe that those things which he saith shall come to pass; he shall have whatsoever he saith.

Mark 11:22,23

In Mark's Gospel we read how Jesus cursed a fig tree and the next time He and His disciples passed that way it had withered from the roots up. The disciples were astonished, but Jesus told them to have faith in God because anyone who did so would be able to do what He had done to the fig tree, (Mark 11:13,14,20-23) and even **...greater works than these shall he do...**(John 14:12).

So from these and other passages in the Bible we see that not only did Jesus live by faith but that He intends and expects us to live that way too.

If our God is a faith Being, and if He made mankind in His own image and likeness, then it is obvious that He meant for man to be a creature of faith. God intended for Adam and Eve to live by faith. Faith in what? Faith in His Word. That's why He walked and talked with Adam in the cool of the evening. He expected Adam's life to be sustained by His Word. He expected him to take authority and exercise dominion over the earth and to operate just as He operated — by faith.

That is why God is displeased when men and women draw back from following the lifestyle of faith that He created, designed and intended for them as the divinely instituted stewards of His whole creation.

A Lifestyle of Faith

And God saw that the wickedness of man was great in the earth, and that every imagination of the thoughts of his heart was only evil continually.

And it repented the Lord that he had made man on the earth, and it grieved him at his heart.

And the Lord said, I will destroy man whom I have created from the face of the earth; both man, and beast,

and the creeping thing, and the fowls of the air; for *it repenteth me that I have made them.*

But Noah found grace in the eyes of the Lord.
Genesis 6:5-8

What God had intended to do in the beginning was to create a continuous lifestyle of faith in the earth, starting with Adam. However, we know that lifestyle was interrupted by sin. The Bible reveals to us that when Adam committed high treason against God, man's nature was altered. It was changed from life to death, spiritual death. Man's faith was perverted to fear. His righteousness, his right standing with God, was perverted to condemnation and a sense of inferiority.

At one time he walked and talked with God face to face, but as soon as he sinned, he felt shame and fear. When God came looking for him, calling, "Where are you?" Adam answered, "I hid myself because I was afraid." (Gen. 3:9,10.)

Now the man and his wife are no longer operating by faith, but by fear. The continuous lifestyle of faith that God had intended for mankind was interrupted by sin so that by the time we get to Genesis chapter 6 we find almost no one who is following this way of life.

A Man of Faith

These are the generations of Noah: *Noah was a just man and perfect in his generations, and Noah walked with God.*

And Noah begat three sons, Shem, Ham, and Japheth.

The earth also was corrupt before God, and the earth was filled with violence.

And God looked upon the earth, and, behold, it was corrupt; for all flesh had corrupted his way upon the earth.

And God said unto Noah, The end of all flesh is come before me; for the earth is filled with violence through them; and, behold, I will destroy them with the earth.

Make thee an ark....

Genesis 6:9-14

Notice that with one lone exception, no one on earth was thinking the thoughts of God. Other than Noah, no one was following the kind of continuous lifestyle of faith that God had instituted when He created Adam and Eve. Instead, the thoughts of men and women were continually evil. They had turned themselves over totally to carnal-mindedness, which the Scriptures tell us is spiritual death. (Rom. 8:6.)

In the whole world there was only one man who was perfect, one man who was walking in fellowship with God and in dominion over the earth as God had intended. All the rest of creation had corrupted their way and had turned to violence and evil. So the Lord decided to destroy the earth but to preserve Noah and his family and the animals that He instructed Noah to carry into the ark with him.

What God was doing was purging the earth and starting all over with Noah and his sons. He was once again making an effort to establish and preserve an ongoing lineage of faith in the earth.

Go Forth and Multiply

And God spake unto Noah, saying,

Go forth of the ark, thou, and thy wife, and thy sons, and thy sons' wives with thee.

Bring forth with thee every living thing that is with thee, of all flesh, both of fowl, and of cattle, and of every creeping thing that creepeth upon the earth; that they may breed abundantly in the earth, and *be fruitful, and multiply* upon the earth.

And Noah went forth, and his sons, and his wife, and his sons' wives with him:

Every beast, every creeping thing, and every fowl, and whatsoever creepeth upon the earth, after their kinds, went forth out of the ark.

Genesis 8:15-19

After the flood God instructed Noah and his family to go forth from the ark along with all the animals and to be fruitful and multiply upon the earth.

Here God was beginning again after the failure of His covenant with Adam and Eve had caused an interruption in His planned lineage of faith.

While the Earth Remaineth

And Noah builded an altar unto the Lord; and took of every clean beast, and of every clean fowl, and offered burnt offerings on the altar.

And the Lord smelled a sweet savour; and the Lord said in his heart, I will not again curse the ground any more for man's sake; for the imagination of man's heart is evil from his youth; neither will I again smite any more every thing living, as I have done.

While the earth remaineth, seedtime and harvest, and cold and heat, and summer and winter, and day and night shall not cease.

Genesis 8:20-22

After Noah and his family came forth from the ark, Noah took some of the clean animals and sacrificed them to the Lord in thanksgiving for their safe voyage.

Seeing this act of obedience on the part of Noah, the Lord determined within Himself that He would never again destroy all living things on the earth by a flood. He began to make a plan for the reinstitution of a covenant with man that would go on forever, one that would last during "seedtime and harvest, and cold and heat, and summer and winter, and day and night" as long as "the earth remaineth."

A New Beginning

And God blessed Noah and his sons, and said unto them, *Be fruitful, and multiply,* and replenish the earth.

And the fear of you and the dread of you shall be upon every beast of the earth, and upon every fowl of the air, upon all that moveth upon the earth, and upon all the fishes of the sea; into your hand are they delivered....

And you, *be ye fruitful, and multiply;* bring forth abundantly in the earth, and multiply therein.

Genesis 9:1,2,7

Does any of that terminology sound familiar? Certainly! It sounds just like what God had originally said to Adam. God said the same things to Noah that He said to Adam because in God's mind this was the inauguration of a new beginning on the earth.

God was expecting Noah to live the kind of faith life He had expected Adam to live. What's more, He was expecting Noah to teach it to his sons so it would be carried on to succeeding generations. Why? Because God knew that one day His Son Jesus Christ would be returning to the earth and would be seeking a lineage of faith. And you and I are part of that lineage!

A Generational Faith

And God spake unto Noah, and to his sons with him, saying,

And I, behold, I establish my covenant with you, and *with your seed after you.*

Genesis 9:8,9

Notice here's how God thinks. He doesn't think in terms of one generation. He is a visionary. He thinks in terms of multiple generations.

Most of the time in the Bible you will find God speaking in terms of at least three generations: "I am the God of Abraham, and of Isaac, and of Jacob." I believe the reason is this: once a lifestyle is adopted by at least three consecutive generations of people, there is a strong likelihood that it will be perpetuated.

If God can get me to live by faith and my children to live by faith, and my children's children to live by faith, it is likely that from now until Jesus comes, the Savelle household will be people of faith.

God's plan was for Noah to father and foster faith in his children and his grandchildren so God could preserve a lineage of faith on the earth.

Perpetual Faith

And God said, This is the token of the covenant which I make between me and you and every living creature that is with you, *for perpetual generations.*

Genesis 9:12

God made a covenant with Noah and his sons and with **every living creature...for** *perpetual* **generations.**

I am a word study person. When I study I have many translations and concordances spread out all over the table. Most of the time when I study the Word of God, a phrase or word will stand out to me, and I will pursue a study of that word like a hidden treasure to see what the Lord is endeavoring to show me.

The word that stood out to me in Genesis 9:12 was *perpetual*. According to the dictionary, there are a number of definitions of this word: 1) "lasting or enduring forever or for an indefinitely long time," 2) "continuing indefinitely without interruption," 3) "unceasing" and 4) "constant."[1]

If we insert these definitions into this verse, we see that the covenant God is making with Noah is intended to last forever. It is to continue indefinitely without interruption and be unceasing and constant.

God wanted every generation after Noah to be made aware of this covenant. If Noah failed to preach it to his sons, and if his sons failed to preach it to their sons, then the earth would become void of the knowledge of the covenant.

It was important that Noah preach the terms of the covenant to those of his family who would live on after he was gone. If God's covenant had been known to only Noah's generation, then after that generation had died out, God would have been forgotten in the earth.

---

[1] *Webster's New World Dictionary*, 3rd college ed., s.v. "perpetual."

Therefore, it was important to God that it be passed on from father to son perpetually — without interruption, continuing, unceasing.

A New Generation of Faith

As we have seen, when Adam sinned, the life of faith that God had initiated with him was interrupted by high treason — to the point that every man on planet earth was so evil and his thoughts so corrupted continually that God was sorry that He had made man.

Instead of allowing the situation to continue in this vein, God destroyed mankind and all the living creatures on the earth by a flood except for Noah and his house and two of every beast. Because Noah had found grace in God's eyes, the Lord chose him to start a new generation of faith.

Noah's obedience in building the ark over a lengthy period of time in spite of ridicule and opposition was a great act of faith. Because of his act of obedience, he and his entire family were saved from destruction.

After the flood, the first thing that God does is to enter into covenant with Noah. He tells him that as long as the earth remains, this covenant will be in force. It will be for perpetual generations.

But did you notice that God never refers to Noah as "the father of faith"? That title will be later conferred on a man named Abram. Noah demonstrated a great *act* of faith. However, his actions after the flood do not reveal a consistent *lifestyle* of faith.

I believe the reason Noah was not called the father of faith is because he was not successful in perpetuating the lifestyle of faith through his children and their descendants.

Noah's Responsibility

Now these are the generations of the sons of Noah, Shem, Ham, and Japheth: and u*nto them were sons born after the flood*....

These are the families of the sons of Noah, after their generations, in their nations: and by these were the nations divided in the earth after the flood.

Genesis 10:1,32

Here we see that after the flood Noah's sons produced sons of their own. These sons then went on to produce sons, and a huge family was eventually formed.

All these people were the direct descendants of one man — Noah. As such, Noah was directly responsible for seeing that they were informed about the perpetual covenant that the Lord had made with them through him. Let's look to see how well Noah succeeded in handling this awesome responsibility.

Noah's Failure

And the whole earth was of one language, and of one speech.

And it came to pass, as they journeyed from the east, that they found a plain in the land of Shinar; and they dwelt there.

And they said one to another, Go to, let us make brick, and burn them thoroughly. And they had brick for stone, and slime had they for mortar.

And they said, Go to, *let us build us a city and a tower, whose top may reach unto heaven;* and *let us make us a name*, lest we be scattered abroad upon the face of the whole earth.

> **And the Lord came down to see the city and the tower, which the children of men builded.**
>
> **And the Lord said, Behold, the people is one, and they have all one language; and this they begin to do: and now nothing will be restrained from them, which they have imagined to do.**
>
> **Go to, let us go down, and there confound their language, that they may not understand one another's speech.**
>
> **So the Lord scattered them abroad from thence upon the face of all the earth: and they left off to build the city.**
>
> **Genesis 11:1-8**

Here — just two chapters after the account of the flood — we see that Noah's family, his sons and their sons, are no longer pursuing Jehovah God. Instead, they are building themselves a tower to heaven. They are trying to erect their own system of religion.

So although Noah was a great man of faith who is listed in the Hebrews 11 Faith Hall of Fame, he did not demonstrate a lifestyle of faith because he did not perpetuate it in his sons and their descendants.

3

The Heritage of Faith

Now the Lord had said unto Abram, Get thee out of thy country, and from thy kindred, and from thy father's house, unto a land that I will shew thee:

And I will make of thee a great nation, and I will bless thee, and make thy name great; and thou shalt be a blessing:

And I will bless them that bless thee, and curse him that curseth thee: and *in thee shall all families of the earth be blessed.*

Genesis 12:1-3

Here we see God thinking as a visionary again. He is thinking about generations, about a lifestyle that He wants Abram not only to demonstrate, but also to perpetuate.

When God dealt with Abram, He was looking into the future. His purpose was not just to bless Abram, but to bless **all families of the earth** — including yours and mine!

Since God is a visionary, He doesn't stop with one generation. He is looking for a way to bless all people everywhere, throughout the ages.

We see the life of Abraham detailed in both the Old Testament and the New Testament. Many of the times that faith is mentioned in the New Testament we see Abraham's name connected with it.

Why did God record everything that Abraham did? Because He wanted to establish a *heritage of faith*.

God wants you and me to live by faith not just because it works, but because He is establishing a heritage. For us to draw back is to do dishonor to our heritage.

So Shall Thy Seed Be

After these things the word of the Lord came unto Abram in a vision, saying, Fear not, Abram: I am thy shield, and thy exceeding great reward.

And Abram said, Lord God, what wilt thou give me, seeing I go childless....

And Abram said, Behold, to me thou hast given no seed: and, lo, one born in my house is mine heir.

And, behold, the word of the Lord came unto him, saying, This shall not be thine heir; but he that shall come forth out of thine own bowels shall be thine heir.

And he brought him forth abroad, and said, Look now toward heaven, and tell the stars, if thou be able to number them: and he said unto him, *So shall thy seed be*.

And he believed in the Lord; and he counted it to him for righteousness.

Genesis 15:1-6

Abram had to have faith in God in order to perpetuate faith. In fact, since his wife was barren, he had to have faith even to *get* a child to whom he could pass on this lifestyle of faith! And that is exactly what he did. When the Lord took him out under the stars and told him, **So shall thy seed be,** Abram laid hold onto that word and refused to let go of it.

But that alone is not the real reason Abraham became known as "the father of faith." Noah also believed God, yet he was not given this title. What did Abraham do that Noah did not do?

The Father of Faith

And the Lord said, Shall I hide from Abraham that thing which I do [destroy Sodom and Gomorrah];

Seeing that Abraham shall surely become a great and mighty nation, and all the nations of the earth shall be blessed in him?

For I know him, that *he will command his children and his household after him, and they shall keep the way of the Lord,* **to do justice and judgment; that the Lord may bring upon Abraham that which he hath spoken of him.**

Genesis 18:17-19

Here we see the Lord saying, "The reason I have chosen this man Abraham is because I know him. He will command this lifestyle of faith to his children and to his children's children."

Abraham is called "the father of faith" not simply because he exercised faith in God, but because he perpetuated that faith through his descendants. This is where Noah failed. Although Noah acted in faith during his own lifetime, he failed to perpetuate that life of faith in his sons and their sons after them.

Just as God intended for Noah to teach this lifestyle of faith to his sons, so He intended for Abraham to teach it to his son Isaac, and for Isaac to teach it to his son Jacob, and for Jacob to teach it to his sons. That was part of God's plan to create a lineage of faith in the earth so that when Jesus came He could see that lineage and know the people He was coming for.

Jesus and the Life of Faith

And when Jesus was entered into Capernaum, there came unto him a centurion, beseeching him,

And saying, Lord, my servant lieth at home sick of the palsy, grievously tormented.

And Jesus saith unto him, I will come and heal him.

The centurion answered and said, Lord, I am not worthy that thou shouldest come under my roof: but speak the word only, and my servant shall be healed....

When Jesus heard it, he marvelled, and said to them that followed, Verily I say unto you, I have not *found* so great *faith*, no, *not in Israel*.

Matthew 8:5-8,10

Although God had instituted a lineage of faith and had found a man, Abraham, through whom this lifestyle could be perpetuated for future generations, by the time Jesus came in the flesh, that lifestyle of faith was again almost non-existent. He could hardly find it anywhere, not even in Israel among the direct descendants of Abraham — the father of faith. That's the reason Jesus said, **O faithless generation** (Mark 9:19).

So faced with this situation, Jesus set about to re-establish the faith line Himself. He took twelve men and began to instruct them and to impart faith into their lives. Why? Because He had not given up on God's plan. He knew that He was going to come back someday looking for faith — and when He did, He intended to find it!

The Successors to Jesus

Later, after Pentecost, we see the effects of Jesus' efforts. We see Peter, for example, acting just like Him.

If we could have followed Peter around, we would have thought that we were seeing Jesus. He was bold, like Jesus. He healed, like Jesus. He walked in authority, like Jesus. He cast out devils, like Jesus. He even started teaching the lifestyle of faith to others, just as Jesus had done.

Then God found a fellow named Saul of Tarsus. He gave him the "Damascus road experience," imparted the lifestyle of faith to him and changed his name from Saul to Paul.

This man started acting like Jesus, too. He walked in his authority and preached, "The just shall live by faith!"

The devil, however, knew that he couldn't take such developments lying down. He realized that if this lineage of faith were established, it would control his operations in the earth. So he fought back by trying to convince these new believers to turn faith from a lifestyle into a religious term.

Eventually he succeeded in getting the Word of God completely out of the hands of ordinary men and hidden away in monasteries. The absence of God's Word during that time gave birth to what history calls the Dark Ages.

But God raised up a man named Martin Luther.

Luther started digging around in those places where the Word of God was hidden, and he came out preaching, "The just shall live by faith!"

Once again, God was establishing a lineage. After Luther, men like John Wesley and Charles Finney came along. Then a seventeen-year-old boy whom God raised up from his deathbed while reading his Methodist grandmother's Bible heard God say, "Go and teach My people faith!"

And, thank God, Kenneth Hagin obeyed. He preached faith even when people ridiculed him and spoke out against him. He preached it when others wrote books and articles critical of him. No matter what happened, he just kept preaching faith.

As he did, people started catching hold of faith and living by it. One of them was a fellow by the name of Kenneth Copeland. He got so stirred up about it, he began preaching faith himself!

God sent him to Shreveport, Louisiana, where a young man named Jerry Savelle was wasting away in a paint and body shop. He grabbed hold of the lifestyle of faith, and his whole life turned upside down.

The same thing could be said about literally thousands of men and women in the last twenty years. No wonder the devil is so stirred up over the faith message! God has finally gotten His lineage! And this time it is not going to be interrupted. This time it is going to be perpetual!

The Heritage of Faith!

Simon Peter, a servant and an apostle of Jesus Christ, to them that have obtained *like precious faith* with us through the righteousness of God and our Saviour Jesus Christ.

2 Peter 1:1

As I travel around the country these days, I meet grown men and women who attended faith meetings as children fifteen years ago. They are living the life of faith now because their mothers and fathers lived it back then.

Faith is our heritage! We don't live the life of faith because it is a fad, or a movement. We live it because it is our heritage.

My ancestors lived this way. When I read the Bible, I don't look at Abraham and Isaac and Jacob as Bible characters only. They are my spiritual ancestors. They lived by faith before I did. I owe it to my heritage to live this way.

I believe that is the reason that Peter called this faith **precious**. It is a spiritual heirloom passed down from one generation to another. That's why we are told in Hebrews 10:35, **Cast not away therefore your confidence** [your precious heritage of faith], **which hath great recompence of reward.**

My wife Carolyn has a heritage that is precious. When she was just a baby, she was taken by her parents to Oral Roberts' tent meetings where she was laid on the sawdust floors. As a child, she witnessed not only Brother Roberts' tent meetings, but also the early meetings of men like Gordon Lindsay and William Branham. She saw miracles, signs and wonders and witnessed the moving of God's Spirit through some of the pioneers of the Pentecostal message in America. She has a wonderful heritage in the things of God.

When she was eight years old she was saved, filled with the Spirit and called to preach. She made a vow then that she would serve the Lord and preach the Gospel. She also vowed that the man she married

37

would be born again and filled with the Holy Ghost, and that he would one day preach the Gospel and go to Africa. When she told me these things the day before our wedding, I informed her that she was marrying the wrong man.

"No, I'm not," she said, "you're the man!"

And, of course, that is exactly what has happened.

I have in my possession some family heirlooms that have been passed down for generations. These heirlooms are priceless, precious treasures to me. They are a part of my heritage.

In the same way, the life of faith is an heirloom that must be passed on from one generation to another. It is my responsibility to pass down this precious heritage to my children. My life before them must be an example of faith. I am held responsible by God not only for passing the life of faith to my children, but also for seeing to it that they, in turn, pass it down to their children.

When my grandsons were born, I had them in my arms within twenty minutes, blessing them and talking to them about their heritage. Today my oldest grandson is almost five years old. His heroes are all faith preachers. When Kenneth Copeland comes on television, he stands right in front of the screen, listening to every word. Then he kisses Brother Copeland before he goes off the air.

His hero is not some rock 'n' roll star or television celebrity — it's a preacher of faith. You may say, "Yes, but he's just a little kid." That's right! We are starting him young. There is a precious heritage involved here, just as there is a precious heritage that needs to be passed down in your family from generation to generation.

I know you may have had struggles with faith in the past. You may have allowed adverse circumstances, bad experiences or the negative opinions of other people to virtually convince you that the faith life is not the way to live.

But once this faith message drops into your spirit, there is no circumstance or experience that can turn you away from it, and no demon in hell that can talk you out of it — ever again.

One of these days, when Jesus comes back and says, "I'm looking for that rare thing called faith," you and I will be able to declare, "Look no farther, Lord! Here we are! We live faith! It's our heritage — our very precious heritage — and, thank God, this time we didn't let go of it!"

4
The Reward of Faith

Cast not away therefore your confidence [your precious heritage of faith], **which hath great** *recompence of reward.*

For ye have need of patience, that, after ye have done the will of God, ye might receive the promise.

Hebrews 10:35,36

Obviously, there is a reward that accompanies the lifestyle of faith which the Lord requires of His children, as we see even more clearly in *The Living Bible* translation of this passage:

Do not let this happy trust in the Lord die away, no matter what happens. *Remember your reward!* **You need to keep on patiently doing God's will if you want him to do for you all that he has promised.**

But as we have seen, the writer of Hebrews also warns us that if we are to reap this reward and receive all that God has promised us, we must be careful to remain firm and to not draw back.

Don't Draw Back!

Now the just shall live by faith: but *if any man draw back, my soul shall have no pleasure in him.*

But we are not of them who draw back unto perdition; but of them that believe to the saving of the soul.

Hebrews 10:38,39

The Amplified Bible renders these verses:

> **But the just shall live by faith [My righteous servant shall live by his conviction respecting man's relationship to God and divine things, and holy fervor born of faith and conjoined with it]; and *if he draws back and shrinks in fear, My soul has no delight or pleasure in him.***
>
> **But our way is not that of those who draw back to eternal misery (perdition) and are utterly destroyed, but we are of those who believe [who cleave to and trust in and rely on God through Jesus Christ, the Messiah] and by faith preserve the soul.**

What the writer is saying here is, "I have drawn a line in my life and I refuse to step back from it. For me to do so would be to compromise what I know to be true from the Word of God."

Here we get a picture of Satan standing on the other side of that line of faith throwing temptations at the believer, trying desperately to convince him that it is pointless to keep standing in faith on God's Word of promise. The devil will hover near that line trying to raise fear and doubt in the heart of the one who has taken a position of faith. He knows that if he can cause the believer to compromise in the least, he will win the victory over him.

This picture reminds me of when I was a child growing up in Louisiana. When the boys in our school got into a fight with one another, they would draw a line in the dirt and dare each other to cross it.

One time I saw a couple of youngsters get into an argument and square off to fight it out. One of them drew a line in the dirt and said, "If you cross that line, I'm gonna bust you right in the lip!" The other kid just stood there shaking like a leaf. He was too scared to cross that line. Finally, he turned and took off for home, crying as he went.

From that experience, I got the idea, "Boy, if I ever get into a fight, I'm gonna draw me a line!"

So one day a big bully began picking on me. I remembered what I had seen and drew a line on the ground right in front of him. I told him, "I dare you to cross that line." He stepped over it like it wasn't there. He got right up in my face, so I stepped back and drew another line. He stepped over that one too. I drew another and another, and he stepped over them also — until he had backed me up against the school building where I couldn't draw any more lines.

You see, I had overlooked one thing: I wasn't serious about my lines — and the bully knew it.

That's what the devil will do to us, if we let him. He will step right over our lines and intimidate us with sickness or poverty or catastrophe or anything it takes to make us back down and give up without a fight. One way or another, Satan is going to put us to the test to see if we are really serious about taking a stand of faith and not drawing back. If we have any tendency at all to compromise, the devil will soon find it out. And so will the Lord.

Our heavenly Father is longsuffering, but He has declared that He has no pleasure in those who take a stand and then draw back from it. On the other hand, it pleases God when He finds a person who will stand firm in faith. Hebrews 11:6 tells us that **without faith it is impossible to please him** [God].

We cannot please the Lord if we do not live by faith. But even if we live by faith, we will not be pleasing to Him if we fail to pass down to future generations the marvelous heritage of faith that has been bestowed upon us.

A Faithless Generation

And when the Lord saw it, he abhorred them, because of the provoking of his sons, and of his daughters.

And he said, I will hide my face from them, *I will see what their end shall be*: **for they are a very froward generation, children in whom is no faith.**

Deuteronomy 32:19,20

Here the Lord is saying, "When men do not live this lifestyle of faith and do not pass down this precious heritage of faith to their children, they are a disobedient, rebellious generation who is not going to enjoy the privileges that come from the faith life."

There are many people who want the benefits of living by faith, but who don't want the discipline of the faith life. They want to reap the rewards, to receive all that God has promised them, but they don't want to make the commitment it takes to reap those rewards.

There are many benefits that come as a result of serving God. The psalmist tells us to **...forget not all his benefits** (Ps. 103:2). There are rewards for serving the Lord, although that should not be our motivation in serving Him. There are blessings that come from living by faith. But in order to reap those benefits and enjoy these blessings, we must be willing to make the commitments involved.

One of those commitments is patience. Nothing happens overnight. Everything takes time. That's why the writer of Hebrews tells us that it is by faith and patience that we inherit the promises of God. (Heb. 6:12.)

The opposite of patience is impatience, and the opposite of faith is fear. Just as faith comes by hearing the Word of God (Rom. 10:17), so fear comes by hearing the word of Satan. Fear, like faith, is released by words and actions.

In Hebrews 11:1 we read that **...faith is the substance of things hoped for, the evidence of things not seen.** So then, just as faith is the substance of things hoped for, fear is the substance of things feared. Job said, **...the thing which I greatly feared is come upon me, and that which I was afraid of is come unto me** (Job 3:25). If fear has the power to bring upon us that which we greatly dread, what do you suppose will be brought upon us if we greatly believe?

I have a saying: "The thing which I greatly 'faithed' is come upon me."

Fear and faith are opposite forces. Just as it is impossible to please God without faith, it is impossible to please Satan without fear.

Fear attracts the devil just as faith attracts God. If we are a people without faith, then we are obviously a people with fear. If we do not have God in our life, then we have the devil in our life. That's what God was saying of this people in Deuteronomy 32:20: "They are children who have no faith. They are being dictated to, ordered about and controlled by Satan."

That same thing can happen to us, if we allow it. But the moment we begin to operate in faith, God is brought onto the scene and the situation begins to change. God wants to be involved in every aspect of our lives. But for Him to get involved, we must have faith.

Notice that Hebrews 11:6 doesn't say that it is impossible to please God without religion. Neither does it say that it is impossible to please God without tradition. Nor does it say that it is impossible to please God without philosophy. It says that it is impossible to please God without *faith*.

When God sees a people in whom there is no faith, like those described in Deuteronomy 32:20, His hands are tied. He has to stand by and watch what happens to them, because they have not invited Him in on the scene by developing and perpetuating an unwavering, uncompromising faith in Him.

Developing and Perpetuating a Lifestyle of Faith

Hear therefore, O Israel, and observe to do it; *that it may be well with thee*, and that ye may increase mightily, as the Lord God of thy fathers hath promised thee, in the land that floweth with milk and honey.

Hear, O Israel: The Lord our God is one Lord:

And thou shalt love the Lord thy God with all thine heart, and with all thy soul, and with all thy might.

And these words, which I command thee this day, shall be in thine heart:

And *thou shalt teach them diligently unto thy children*, and shalt talk of them when thou sittest in thine house, and when thou walkest by the way, and when thou liest down, and when thou risest up.

Deuteronomy 6:3-7

What is God endeavoring to do here? He is endeavoring to pass down a heritage — a spiritual heritage.

When children grow up in a home in which there is darkness because God's Word is not lived and taught, it is not unusual to find these same children establishing homes just like the one from which they came. This negative heritage of darkness, ungodliness and perverseness gets passed down from one generation to the next.

There is an old saying: "Like father, like son." It means, of course, that in time most young people end up being very much like their parents.

I have been amazed lately at all the TV talk shows in which people reveal how they were abused as children. Most of them will say, "When I was being abused, I thought to myself, 'When I grow up and have children of my own, I'll never do this to them!'"

Yet, sadly, many of them can't help themselves. They wind up mistreating their children just as they were mistreated by their parents. Why does that happen? Because the curse has never been broken. The lineage has never been changed from one of sin to one of faith.

Some people talk about certain family maladies or conditions such as heart disease, cancer or diabetes. Some even seem to be absolutely convinced that they are going to die from the same sickness that killed their parents or relatives — and many times, sadly enough, that proves to be the case. The conclusion is, of course, that "it's just in the genes." As believers, you and I don't have in us the genes of fear and death, we have the genes of faith and life! These are the genes God expects us to pass on to our children and grandchildren.

Here in this passage He is instructing the Children of Israel, "Pass My words on to your children. Create in them a heritage of faith." In verse 7 He instructs parents to speak His words when they are sitting in their houses, when they are walking along the way, when they get up in the morning and when they go to bed at night. What is He getting at here? He is saying that these people are to demonstrate not just a Sabbath day faith, but an everyday lifestyle of faith.

As the children of God, you and I are to create and demonstrate a lifestyle of faith in our homes.

In many families, the children see Christianity demonstrated only on Sundays and special occasions. The only time they see their parents praying is just before a meal. The only time they see them reading the Bible is on Saturday night in last-minute preparation for Sunday school the next day. The only time they hear them speaking of the Lord is when the pastor comes to pay a visit. Most children who see such a double standard being set before them grow up not wanting to have anything to do with that kind of empty, hypocritical lifestyle.

That's why it is so important that we Christian parents develop and maintain a consistent lifestyle of faith — and then pass it on to our children and grandchildren. It is such a joy to know that this precious heritage is being perpetuated. There is also a reward that goes with it.

Pass on the Heritage of Faith, Receive the Blessings of the Lord

And thou shalt bind them for a sign upon thine hand, and they shall be as frontlets between thine eyes.

> And thou shalt write them upon the posts of thy house, and on thy gates.
>
> And it shall be, when the Lord thy God shall have brought thee into the land which he sware unto thy fathers, *to Abraham, to Isaac, and to Jacob,* to give thee great and goodly cities, which thou buildedst not,
>
> And *houses full of all good things,* which thou filledst not, and wells digged, which thou diggedst not, vineyards and olive trees, which thou plantedst not; when thou shalt have eaten and be full;
>
> Then beware lest thou forget the Lord, which brought thee forth out of the land of Egypt, from the house of bondage.
>
> Deuteronomy 6:8-12

Notice the three-generation heritage mentioned here: Abraham, Isaac and Jacob. God is saying to His people: "This is the way Abraham lived, the way Isaac lived and the way Jacob lived. Everything I promised and provided for them I will give to you. I will give you houses full of good things, wells of pure water, vineyards and fruit trees and everything you need for a full and happy life."

Our two daughters know what it is like to live a lifestyle of faith. Many's the time they came home from school to find that their parents had given away clothing or furniture or cars because the Lord had instructed them to do so. But they also saw those same things or even better things returned to us by the Lord because we had been obedient to Him. Our girls had many opportunities to watch God do what He does best — keep His Word.

Because they grew up that way, they live that way.

Since Carolyn and I were ministers, we seemed to get on the mailing list of just about every preacher in the country, and some of them used every kind of gimmick and trick in the world to get people to send them money. I didn't want my children growing up thinking that living by faith meant playing up to the right people, resorting to flattery or deceit, dropping hints or running a religious con game.

What the Lord is talking about here in Deuteronomy 6 is not broadcasting our needs, it is professing His power and provision. It is speaking His Word and demonstrating the lifestyle of faith, twenty-four hours a day, seven days a week.

When you talk, talk faith. When you get up, talk faith. When you lie down, talk faith. Whenever you open your mouth to speak, talk faith.

What are the results?

When you and I have demonstrated this kind of lifestyle of faith before our family and have passed this heritage of faith down to our children and grandchildren, the Lord has promised that He will bring us into a place in which everything we need will be provided for us.

But notice that the Lord says that when this reward comes upon us, we are to be careful lest we forget the Lord our God Who brought us out of bondage. We must keep reminding ourselves and our children that we wouldn't have a thing if it were not for God. Like the Children of Israel, without the Lord we would still be living in bondage.

Pass It On!

Give ear, O my people, to my law: incline your ears to the words of my mouth.

I will open my mouth in a parable: I will utter dark sayings of old:

Which we have heard and known, and our fathers have told us.

We will not hide them from their children, shewing to the generation to come the praises of the Lord, and his strength, and his wonderful works that he hath done.
Psalm 78:1-4

Notice how important it is for each generation to pass on to the next generation knowledge of the praises and power and provision of the Lord.

Teach Your Children To Have Faith

For he established a testimony in Jacob, and appointed *a law in Israel, which he commanded our fathers, that they should make them known to their children*:

That the generation to come might know them, even the children which should be born; who should arise and declare them to their children:

That they might set their hope in God, and not forget the works of God, but keep his commandments:

And might not be as their fathers, a stubborn and rebellious generation; a generation that set not their heart aright, and whose spirit was not stedfast with God.

The children of Ephraim, being armed, and carrying bows, turned back in the day of battle.

They kept not the covenant of God, and refused to walk in his law;

And forgat his works, and his wonders that he had shewed them.
Psalm 78:5-11

The Lord has commanded that these things be passed down to our children. We are instructed by God not only to demonstrate a lifestyle of faith before them, but also to teach them to live by faith and to walk in the miraculous. Why? So their generation will have hope in the Lord. So they will set their hearts aright and be steadfast. So they will not be like other generations who have gone before them, generations like the children of Ephraim who gave up, turned coward and caved in on the day of battle.

God is saying to us: "Teach your children how to take a stand against adversity. Teach them to live in victory and peace in the very midst of strife and opposition. Teach them how to take the weapons of their warfare and be strong in the Lord, fully clothed in the armor of God, holding the shield of faith and quenching all the fiery darts of the wicked one. Don't allow your children to be like the children of Ephraim who had the weapons and the armor to defeat the enemy, but who gave up under pressure. Teach your children to stand, and having done all, to stand." (Eph. 6:10-18.)

A Seed of Evildoers

Hear, O heavens, and give ear, O earth: for the Lord hath spoken, I have nourished and brought up children, and they have rebelled against me.

The ox knoweth his owner, and the ass his master's crib: but Israel doth not know, my people doth not consider.

Ah sinful nation, a people laden with iniquity, a *seed of evildoers*, children that are corrupters: they have forsaken the Lord, they have provoked the Holy One of Israel unto anger, they are gone away backward.

Isaiah 1:2-4

Notice these children in whom there was a seed of evil. The heritage of faith had not been passed down to them. As a result, they rebelled against it and became evildoers and corrupters. Instead of going forward in faith, they went backward and became backsliders.

That is what will happen to our children and grandchildren unless we are careful to demonstrate a lifestyle of faith in front of them and then see to it that the glorious heritage of faith we have received is passed on to them and to succeeding generations.

Walk in Obedience

For I spake not unto your fathers, nor commanded them in the day that I brought them out of the land of Egypt, concerning burnt offerings or sacrifices:

But this thing commanded I them, saying, Obey my voice, and I will be your God, and ye shall be my people: and *walk ye in all the ways that I have commanded you, that it may be well unto you.*

But they hearkened not, nor inclined their ear, but walked in the counsels and in the imagination of their evil heart, *and went backward, and not forward.*

Jeremiah 7:22-24

If you and I do not continue to walk in faith, we will end up going backward in life. If we keep drawing back and compromising under pressure, we will regress rather than progress. If we want things to go well with us, if we want to reap the reward of faith, then we must learn to walk in faith and obedience — and then to pass on that knowledge to those who come after us.

5

Holding Faith

Nevertheless I tell you the truth; it is expedient for you that I go away: for if I go not away, the Comforter will not come unto you; but if I depart, I will send him unto you.

John 16:7

In this context, the word *expedient* means to "be profit (-able for)."[1] Here, just before His crucifixion, burial, resurrection and departure from the earth, Jesus is telling His disciples that since He is leaving and sending them the Holy Ghost, life will be more profitable for them.

As believers, as those who are filled with the Spirit of God, our lives should be progressively improving.

My life is not getting worse, it's getting better. I'm not saying that I don't have problems to contend with. On the contrary, I have problems all the time. I discovered years ago that faith and problems travel down the same road. But, thank God, faith is the answer to problems. The solution to all the tests and trails we encounter in life is faith in the Word of God.

---

[1]James Strong, *Strong's Exhaustive Concordance of the Bible* (Nashville: Abingdon, 1890), "Greek Dictionary of the Bible," p. 68, entry #4851.

In spite of the problems you may be dealing with, your life should be getting progressively better. When the problems increase, when the attacks of the enemy intensify and the storms of life become more severe, that is no reason to back off from faith. That's all the more reason to lock into faith, because without faith, you are limited. With faith, all things are possible.

Remember: faith is not just a decision or an act, it is a lifestyle. That's why the writer of the book of Hebrews tells us that we must follow the example of those **who through faith and patience inherit the promises of God** (Heb. 6:12).

I don't know about you, but I don't listen to folks who are losers in life. I don't buy books or tapes from those who have no positive experiences with faith. Why should I spend my time listening to someone who is saying, "Faith didn't work for me"? What does that profit me? Nothing.

It seems that some people are just looking for an excuse to quit. That's why they listen to those who tell them that faith doesn't work.

Of course, faith will be put to the test. That's why the Lord warns us that He takes no pleasure in the one who draws back, which tells me that if anyone makes a decision to live by faith, he will have an opportunity to draw back from that decision. Although some people may preach that if you live by faith, you will never have another problem, that is not my message, and it never has been.

In the parable of the sower and the seed, which represents the Word of God, Jesus told His disciples,

"Once the Word is sown, Satan comes immediately to take it away." (Mark 4:15.) If Satan comes immediately, that creates an opportunity for a problem. Peter says that we must be constantly on our guard because the devil roams around **...seeking whom he may devour** (1 Pet. 5:8). That's why we must have our mind made up that he is not going to devour us!

Satan seeks to devour those who have the Word of God in their heart. Why? Because they are dangerous to him; they pose a threat to his kingdom. The more Word you receive, the more dangerous you become to Satan. The more determined you are to live by faith, the greater the threat you pose to your enemy.

If you continue to walk in faith, you will get to the point that every demon in hell knows your name and address. They will put pressure on you to give up and quit. That's why you must stand firm and not draw back.

If you are going to walk by faith, then don't be naive. Don't think that faith works for Jerry Savelle or Kenneth Copeland or Kenneth Hagin just because we are preachers of the Gospel. No, faith works for us for the same reason it will work for you or for anyone else — because we take a stand and absolutely refuse to budge. We have opportunities to draw back daily. Just because we have been in the ministry preaching faith for decades does not mean that we are immune to Satan's attack. We have to resist the devil just like everyone else. We have to watch our mouths, we have to monitor and control what we say, just like any other believer. Watching the words of our mouth has become a part of our faith lifestyle, as it must for you.

Once you and I hear the word of faith, we can never be passive. Never again can we be neutral about it. Either we will love it or we will hate it. Once we have heard it, from that moment on, any time someone mentions it, it will either lift us up or pull us down. Either it will inspire us to hold fast or it will provoke us to draw back.

I have met pastors who started out with the word of faith, built their churches on it and began to grow and increase because they preached it and people saw the results of it. I have also seen some of those same preachers give up that message for one that tickled people's ears, and immediately their ministry started to go downhill.

One pastor invited me to come and preach in his church because it was falling apart. When he asked me why this was happening, I told him, "It's simple, it's because you're not preaching what got you here. In Texas we have a saying: 'Dance with the one that brung you!'"

What I was telling this man was that he had quit walking with the One Who had brought him that far in his ministry. He had begun to flirt with a message that was more popular at the moment. He needed to stick with "It is written."

That is what you and I must do if we are to walk in victory. We must do as the Apostle Paul told his young disciple, Timothy. We must learn to look to our spiritual heritage.

Three Generations of Faith

Paul, an apostle of Jesus Christ by the will of God, according to the promise of life which is in Christ Jesus,

To Timothy, *my dearly beloved son:* **Grace, mercy, and peace, from God the Father and Christ Jesus our Lord.**

I thank God, *whom I serve from my forefathers* **with pure conscience, that without ceasing I have remembrance of thee in my prayers night and day;**

Greatly desiring to see thee, being mindful of thy tears, **that I may be filled with joy;**

When I call to remembrance *the unfeigned faith that is in thee, which dwelt first in thy grandmother Lois, and thy mother Eunice; and I am persuaded that in thee also.*
2 Timothy 1:1-5

Notice how in verse 3 Paul emphasizes the importance of spiritual heredity when he speaks of "God whom I serve from my forefathers." He also emphasizes his own personal part in that spiritual heredity when he calls Timothy his "dearly beloved son."

Notice also the three generations of faith set forth in the last verse of this passage. Paul is reminding young Timothy of his faith heritage which began with his grandmother Lois, continued through his mother Eunice, and now has been passed down to him.

In Acts 16:1 we learn that Timothy's mother was a Jew, but his father was a Greek. This tells us that even though there may be one member of the family in whom there is no faith, if the one member who does have faith will practice it and live it before the household, it can be passed down to the next generation.

If you are a believer, but your spouse is not, these are good verses to hold to as you work to impart your faith to your children and grandchildren.

Timothy had an added advantage. Not only did he have a marvelous heritage of faith from his mother and grandmother, he also had the wonderful privilege of being personally tutored and disciplined in the faith by the great Apostle Paul. If a person can't get faith from following Paul around, something is wrong with him!

My wife and I had the same kind of privilege with Kenneth and Gloria Copeland. In the early days of their ministry, they took us in as young believers and raised us in the Gospel. I traveled with Brother Copeland, driving for him and taking care of his needs. As such, I got to listen to him preach three services a day everywhere we went. I was also responsible for duplicating the messages on tape, which I did in our hotel room after the services. So I heard every message he preached a minimum of three times: in the meetings, in the hotel room as I duplicated them and later in the car as we drove from one place to the next. And then, as if that were not enough, in my personal study time, I literally dissected each of those messages.

Over a period of time, I got to know Brother Copeland's message very well. In addition to watching the man in the pulpit, I also got to watch him in his daily life. I learned a great deal from Kenneth Copeland, which soon became evident to everyone around me.

It's no wonder that when I finally got to preach, everything I said sounded like Kenneth Copeland. I never knew if I was going to get another chance to speak, so every time I stood in front of an audience I preached everything Kenneth Copeland knew in that one message.

Paul wrote to the believers in Corinth, **Be ye followers of me, even as I also am of Christ** (1 Cor. 11:1). In the

Greek, the word translated *followers* is derived from another word meaning "(a *'mimic'*); to *imitate*."[2] So what Paul is telling the Corinthian believers is, "Be imitators or mimics of me, even as I imitate or mimic Christ."

That is the way I was toward Brother Copeland. Now I was not trying to *be* Kenneth Copeland, but I certainly wanted what I saw in his life. I saw in him a relationship with God that I had never experienced in my own life. I saw a boldness in declaring the Word of God that I had never seen before. I saw an excellence and a wisdom in ministry like none I had ever witnessed. And because I wanted these things so much, God placed me in a position to receive this heritage of faith and to pass it on in order to keep it perpetual.

In fact, when Brother Copeland asked me to come to work with him, I remember him calling me out of an audience in a meeting and prophesying over me: "The Lord has showed me that you and I are to be a team, and it is your responsibility to believe for the perfect timing."

When I eventually went to work for Brother Copeland, I traveled with him for nearly three years. Then after a while the Lord began to deal with my heart about launching out into my own ministry. I really didn't want to do that. I kept reminding the Lord, "You said that You put Brother Copeland and me together as a team. If I leave and start my own ministry, we will no longer be a team."

"Yes, you will," the Lord answered. "I will enable you to cover twice as much territory with the same message."

---

[2] Strong, p. 48, entries #3401, #3402.

That's what God was doing — perpetuating the message.

Since that time I have had many opportunities to draw back. But I made up my mind that I would not quit. I said to myself, "This is the only thing I ever got hold of in my life that works. Why draw back now? Why quit as long as it's working?"

I held firm and refused to draw back from the faith heritage that had been passed down to me from Kenneth Copeland who had inherited it from Kenneth Hagin and Oral Roberts. Like Timothy, I was the third generation of a lineage of faith.

You see, there is a heritage involved here. Paul wrote to Timothy: "I want to stir up your remembrance. You have a heritage to uphold. It started with your grandmother and then was passed to your mother, and now I am persuaded it is in you."

No wonder Paul spent so much time with this young man, instructing him, correcting him, encouraging him — even rebuking him, if necessary. Why? Because he wanted the lifestyle of faith to be perpetuated in Timothy so it would be passed down to the men who would come under Timothy's influence and thus be carried on right down to our generation.

Satan realized how powerful that plan was, so he set out to spoil it. As we have seen, he saw that the only way he could stop the lifestyle of faith from being perpetuated in the earth was to get the Word of God out of the hands of ordinary men. So he managed to get it shut away in monasteries during the Dark Ages.

But we saw how one man, Martin Luther, redis-covered it and began to preach: "The just shall live by faith." It is that same message that burst forth when God ushered in the great outpouring of the Holy Spirit in our generation in what is generally known as the Charismatic Movement.

That is our precious heritage today, one that requires that we "war a good warfare" by "holding faith."

War a Good Warfare

This charge I commit unto thee, son Timothy, according to the prophecies which went before on thee, that thou by them mightest *war a good warfare*;

Holding faith, and a good conscience; which some having put away concerning faith have made shipwreck:

Of whom is Hymenaeus and Alexander; whom I have delivered unto Satan, that they may learn not to blaspheme.

1 Timothy 1:18-20

Notice that it is impossible to "war a good warfare" without "holding faith."

Remember that the man who is writing these words is the same man who has been reminding Timothy of his rich heritage of faith. Now he tells him: "Those prophecies that were spoken over you reveal that God has a plan and a destiny for your life."

God has a plan and a destiny for your life just as much as He did for the life of Timothy. If you ever discover that plan and fulfill that destiny, it will be because you have warred a good warfare.

Warring a good warfare is not easy. It's not tiptoeing through the tulips. This is an all-out, no-holds-barred type warfare waged by a determined, ruthless enemy. But you are prepared and equipped for it. You have the armor of God and the sword of the Spirit, which is the Word of God. (Eph. 6:13-17.) You have the promise of God that no weapon that is formed against you shall prosper. (Is. 54:17.) And you have supernatural help. Remember: only one third of the angelic host fell with Satan. That means that two-thirds of them are still on your side and available upon request. Besides all that, you have the powerful archangel Michael, the war angel, who will come to your rescue if necessary.

If you are to fulfill your divine destiny, you must be prepared to engage in spiritual warfare. The blessings of the Lord don't come easily or automatically. They are not going to just fall upon you from heaven like a ripe apple out of a tree. You are going to have to take your sword, the Word of the living God, and hew your way through the demonic forces that are trying to stop you from receiving God's best in your life. Jesus defeated the devil on the cross so that believers can exercise the authority over Satan Jesus provided for them. You are going to have to stand in that victory, warring a good warfare by "holding faith and a good conscience."

Notice that Paul says that some have failed to do this by "having put away concerning faith." Some have put away this precious thing called faith. And notice the results: they have "made shipwreck." Two examples of those who have made shipwreck of their lives are mentioned by Paul who says that he has delivered them unto Satan "that they may learn not to blaspheme."

I wish Paul were alive today. If he were here, there would be a lot of preachers who would be delivered over unto Satan for blaspheming faith. We're not talking about playing religious games here; this is serious business. I have talked to some people who have been in the faith much longer than I have, and they agree with me than any ministry that blasphemes faith will not be in operation very long.

Believe me, the worst thing you can do is to blaspheme faith. You should never waste time or energy talking negatively about those who teach or preach faith, those who give people hope in life, those who help others to break the yoke of bondage off their necks and free themselves from the devil and his demons.

Remember: it was not a twentieth-century faith preacher who spoke the words recorded in Mark 11:22,23:

> ...Have faith in God.
>
> For verily I say unto you, That whosoever shall say unto this mountain, Be thou removed, and be thou cast into the sea; and shall not doubt in his heart, but shall believe that those things which he saith shall come to pass; he shall have whatsoever he saith.

It was not Kenneth Hagin who was the founder of the faith movement; he got the idea from Jesus. And even Jesus in His earthly ministry was not the first person to demonstrate this lifestyle. As we have seen, the lifestyle of faith has been going on for a long, long time.

This is not some new message that has just surfaced. This is something that God has been endeavoring to get into the hearts of mankind since the Garden of Eden. And it is something that Satan has been trying to destroy since the Garden of Eden. He has done everything he possibly can to silence those who preach and teach it. But no one can silence something that has been initiated by God Himself. He may distract it or hinder it or delay it, but he cannot stop it, because no one can put a halt to what God has ordained.

That's why we must never be guilty of putting away faith and blaspheming it. To do so would be to make shipwreck of our lives. Instead, we must war a good warfare, holding faith and a good conscience, secure in the knowledge that in due season we will reap, if we faint not, if we do not abandon our heritage.

Sell Me Your Birthright!

And when her [Rebekah's] days to be delivered were fulfilled, behold, there were twins in her womb.

And the first came out red, all over like an hairy garment; and they called his name Esau.

And after that came his brother out, and his hand took hold on Esau's heel; and his name was called Jacob: and Isaac was threescore years old when she bare them.

And the boys grew: and Esau was a cunning hunter, a man of the field; and Jacob was a plain man, dwelling in tents.

And Isaac loved Esau, because he did eat of his venison: but Rebekah loved Jacob.

And Jacob sod pottage: and Esau came from the field, and he was faint:

And Esau saith to Jacob, Feed me, I pray thee, with that same red pottage; for I am faint: therefore was his name called Edom.

And Jacob said, *Sell me this day thy birthright.*

And Esau said, *Behold, I am at the point to die: and what profit shall this birthright do to me?*

And Jacob said, Swear to me this day; and he sware unto him: and he sold his birthright unto Jacob.

**Then Jacob gave Esau bread and pottage of lentiles;
and he did eat and drink, and rose up, and went his way:
thus Esau despised his birthright.**

Genesis 25:24-34

See how pressure and weariness can cause a person
to let go of his heritage? Although Esau was the firstborn
and entitled to the greater part of his father's estate, in a
moment of hunger and fatigue he forfeited that valuable
privilege. He allowed a momentary weakness to cloud
his judgment. As a result, he sold his birthright, his
precious heritage, to his brother Jacob for a bowl of
soup and a loaf of bread.

It is when you are wearied from standing in faith,
believing God, when nothing seems to be happening,
that you are most tempted to give up and cave in.
Weariness sets in and the devil comes to whisper in
your ear, "Let's negotiate." He starts to offer you every
incentive in the world to compromise. If you're not
careful you will find yourself doing as Esau did and
saying something like, "What good is this faith, this
Word of God? It's not working anyway, so I may as well
sell it for whatever I can get out of it."

Esau was so weary and hungry that his mind was
affected. He said to himself, "What good is my
birthright if I'm going to die?" His weakened condition
caused him to develop a fatalistic outlook. That's what
fatigue does. It paints a picture of defeat, despair and
discouragement that drops down into your spirit and
affects your judgment and your decision-making
faculties. Like Esau, you begin to ask yourself, "What's
the use of standing any longer? Why hang on anymore?
All this faith stuff is fine for preachers like Jerry Savelle,
Kenneth Copeland and Kenneth Hagin, but it just

doesn't work for me. I'm going to lose anyway, so I may as well give up and get it over with."

That's the way Esau was thinking when he sold his birthright to Jacob for a plate of food. He simply gave into pressure at a time of extreme physical and mental weakness. That happens to many Christians today.

There are a lot of believers who, at some time in the past, laid hold on the word of faith, and even stood firm. Today many of those same people are caving in, selling out and giving up under pressure. They are abandoning their heritage because they are surrendering the good fight of faith.

I like what Kenneth Copeland says: "A good fight is any fight you win."

In the days ahead you are going to have to engage in the good fight of faith. If you stand your ground, you will win. But there will be an opportunity to sell out. You've got to determine in the name of Jesus that your faith is not for sale. It is too costly, too precious, to give up. It is your method of gaining victory over the opposition that comes against you. Whatever the price that is offered for it, don't sell it. Come what may, never sell out.

You must remember to hold faith and a good conscience if you are to avoid making shipwreck of your life.

You and I have a rich heritage of faith. It is our birthright. We must learn to hold onto it in spite of hardships, fatigue and pressure. We must not make Esau's mistake and forfeit our precious birthright for a moment of temporary relief.

6

Resisting Satan

Blessed is the man that walketh not in the counsel of the ungodly, nor standeth in the way of sinners, nor sitteth in the seat of the scornful.

But his delight is in the law of the Lord; and in his law doth he meditate day and night.

And he shall be like a tree planted by the rivers of water, that bringeth forth his fruit in his season; his leaf also shall not wither; and *whatsoever he doeth shall prosper.*

Psalm 1:1-3

How would you like to be at peace, to have everything you do prosper and to be in health? Here is the scriptural key to that blessing. It is to refuse to walk in the counsel of the ungodly, but rather to delight in the law of the Lord and to mediate on it day and night.

This is the walk of faith we have been describing and prescribing. The person who walks by faith is not moved by what others around him may think or say or do because his ears and his eyes, his mind and his heart, are firmly fixed on the Word of the Lord.

The Blessing of the Righteous

Praise ye the Lord. Blessed is the man that feareth the Lord, that delighteth greatly in his commandments.

His seed shall be mighty upon earth: the generation of the upright shall be blessed.

Wealth and riches shall be in his house: and his righteousness endureth for ever.

Unto the upright there ariseth light in the darkness: he is gracious, and full of compassion, and righteous.

A good man sheweth favour, and lendeth: he will guide his affairs with discretion.

Surely he shall not be moved for ever: the righteous shall be in everlasting remembrance.

He shall not be afraid of evil tidings: his heart is fixed, trusting in the Lord.

His heart is established, he shall not be afraid, until he see his desire upon his enemies.

Psalm 112:1-8

Here is another familiar passage that describes the blessings that are kept in reserve for the person who fears the Lord and who walks in faithful obedience to His commandments.

Note that the individual whose mind is firmly fixed on the Lord is not afraid of evil tidings. Bad news does not move him. He does not waver. He is not a compromiser.

In speaking of such a person *The Amplified Bible* often uses the term "the uncompromisingly righteous" or "the consistently righteous."

I would like to suggest that you look up the word *righteous* in the concordance. Locate in the King James translation all the Scriptures that contain this word, and then read them in *The Amplified Bible*. You will discover the many rewards that God promises to the uncompromisingly, consistently righteous, those who walk in faith, refusing to cave in, draw back or sell out, those who will not allow Satan to rob them of their rightful inheritance.

Trust God and Resist the Devil

Humble yourselves therefore under the mighty hand of God, that he may exalt you in due time:

Casting all your cares upon him; for he careth for you.

Be sober, be vigilant; because your adversary the devil, as a roaring lion, walketh about, seeking whom he may devour:

***Whom resist stedfast in the faith,* knowing that the same afflictions are accomplished in your brethren that are in the world.**

1 Peter 5:6-9

In the last chapter we saw how one man in the Bible, Esau, was willing to sell his birthright just to satisfy his physical hunger. Many times that is what happens to believers. Even though they sincerely love God and truly want to stand firm in their faith in Him, they allow their carnal mind to take control over their body. They forfeit their heritage of faith in order to gratify the lusts of their flesh. They look for shortcuts because they are not willing to endure and persevere.

We must be on the alert at all times because, as Peter tells us in this passage, our enemy is out to devour us. Satan is a deceiver, a seducer and a thief. If he can steal our heritage, then he can rob us of the blessings that come from that heritage.

It is obvious from this passage that while you and I are going about our daily lives, our adversary the devil is roaming around, seeking ways to destroy us. That's why we must take a stand and resist him firmly in the faith.

Did you ever play the old childhood game called "May I?" Each time a player wanted to advance, he had to receive permission from the leader by asking, "May I?" That is the way it is with Satan. Each time he seeks to take advantage of us in any way, we must stand firm and tell him, "No, you may not!"

One of the most important times when we have to stand firm in faith is right after a victory. That is usually when we are the most vulnerable. Many times after we have won a great battle we are so worn out that all we want to do is shed the armor of God, drop the shield of faith and lay down the sword of the Spirit in hopes that we won't have to use them for a while.

We have believed God for the impossible so long that when what we have been standing in faith for finally comes to pass, we think, "Thank God, that's over! Now I can relax." That is when we become susceptible to being devoured because our resistance is at its weakest. In such moments we must remember that just because we have won a battle does not mean that we have won the war.

Regardless of our victory, the war is still raging. The enemy is still out there on the field of battle, still plotting his strategy, still devising his tactics, still planning his next attack. That's why we must not let down our guard, even for a moment.

I have got to the place that when I win a battle, I say, "Hallelujah! Thank You, Lord," and then I immediately lift my shield, grab my sword and jump to my feet to stand guard. After a victory, I have learned to be vigilant, to be sober, to be on the alert, because I know that my adversary is going to launch a counterattack — right when I am least prepared.

Notice that, in this passage, Peter tells us how we are to defend ourselves against the devil. When Satan launches his assault against us, when he comes at us to steal, kill and destroy us (John 10.10), the only way we will be able to keep him from devouring us is by resisting him steadfastly in the faith.

There is no room for wavering. To be steadfast requires great determination, great discipline, a great interior drive that will not allow us to quit.

James tells us, **Submit yourselves therefore to God. Resist the devil, and he will flee from you** (James 4:7). I love that verse because I know that the devil doesn't have that promise. Nowhere in the Word of God can Satan find the comfort of knowing that he will be successful. But you and I have the joyful assurance that if we submit ourselves to God and steadfastly resist the enemy, he will flee from us.

Satan is by nature a quitter, so all we have to do is to enforce the law of the Lord against him. The devil has no choice in the matter. He has to quit. Why? Because God has said so: "Resist the devil, and he *will* flee from you." You and I don't have to bow to Satan. We have no obligation whatsoever to flee from him. We have been given weapons to use against him and **...the weapons of our warfare are not carnal, but mighty through God to the pulling down of strong holds** (2 Cor. 10:4).

You and I have been given the whole armor of God, the shield of faith and the sword of the Spirit, which is the Word of God. (Eph. 6:10-17.) Even if we can't think of a particular Scripture to use to resist the devil, we can always use the name of Jesus. Revelation 19:13 tells us that **...his name is called The Word of God**. Whenever we use the name of Jesus against Satan, we have thrown at him the whole book — from Genesis through Revelation — in one word!

The Amplified Bible version of 1 Peter 5:8,9 reads:

> **Be well-balanced (temperate, sober of mind), be vigilant and cautious at all times; for that enemy of yours, the devil, roams around like a lion roaring [in fierce hunger], seeking someone to seize upon and devour.**
>
> **Withstand him; be firm in faith [against his onset — rooted, established, strong, immovable, and determined], knowing that the same (identical) sufferings are appointed to your brotherhood (the whole body of Christians) throughout the world.**

It is vitally important that we be cautious, that we be alert, that we be vigilant where our adversary is concerned. It is equally important that we be knowledgeable about our enemy and his tactics. The Apostle Paul says that we should not be ignorant of Satan's devices. (2 Cor. 2:11.) Let's look at the book of Genesis to discover something about the nature of our enemy to help us understand more clearly how to combat him.

The Nature of Satan

> **Now** *the serpent was more subtil than any beast of the field which the Lord God had made.* **And he said unto the woman, Yea, hath God said, Ye shall not eat of every tree of the garden?**
>
> **Genesis 3:1**

The Bible refers to Satan as a serpent, the most "subtil" creature on earth. The word *subtle* is defined as "crafty," "skilful in deceiving," "insidious."[1]

---

[1]*Funk and Wagnalls New Comprehensive International Dictionary of the English Language,* s.v. "subtle."

That's the reason the Bible tells us that we must be sober, vigilant and alert at all times. Why? Because Satan's greatest weapon, his most effective device, is his subtlety, his craftiness. He is the master deceiver. In fact, the Bible reveals to us from the writings of the Apostle Paul that Satan even has the ability to actually transform himself into an angel of light. (2 Cor. 11:14.) He can sound so convincing that if you and I are not sensitive to the voice of the Lord, if we are not firmly established in the Word of God, we can be deceived.

One of the primary ways the devil deceives the believer is by distorting or perverting the Word of the Lord. In the fourth chapter of Luke we read how he twice said to Jesus, "If You are the Son of God..." (vv. 3,9.) Why did he use those words? Because in the Gospel of Matthew we see that just before this incident, at the moment of Jesus' baptism in the Jordan River, God spoke from heaven and said, **...This is my beloved Son, in whom I am well pleased** (Matt. 3:17). True to his nature, Satan immediately came to tempt Jesus, while He was weak from fasting for forty days and nights, by casting doubt on the Word of God just spoken to Him. That's why he begins his temptations with, "*If* You are the Son of God..." This is the same tactic of casting doubt upon God's Word that Satan used with Eve when he asked her, "Did God *really* say that you are not to eat of the trees of the garden?"

When the devil tempted Jesus by saying, "If You are really the Son of God, command this stone to be turned into bread," Jesus answered him by quoting Scripture: **...It is written, That man shall not live by bread alone, but by every word of God** (Luke 4:4).

Undaunted, the devil then took Jesus to the top of a high mountain and tempted Him again by saying, "If You will fall down and worship me, everything You see will be Yours." Again, Jesus answered by quoting Scripture: **...Get thee behind me, Satan: for it is written, Thou shalt worship the Lord thy God, and him only shalt thou serve** (v. 8).

When the devil heard Jesus say the second time, **It is written**, he must have thought to himself, "Oh, this is one of those 'Word people'!" So in his final temptation, when he took Jesus to the pinnacle of the temple and challenged Him to cast Himself down, he found himself a Scripture to quote: **For it is written, He shall give his angels charge over thee, to keep thee: And in their hands they shall bear thee up, lest at any time thou dash thy foot against a stone** (vv. 10,11).

Of course, God never intended for that passage or any other part of His Word to be used to tempt people into doing wrong. James tells us: **Let no man say when he is tempted, I am tempted of God: for God cannot be tempted with evil, neither tempteth he any man** (James 1:13).

So we see that Satan tries to deceive the believer by distorting or perverting the Word of God. This is especially true of those who call themselves "Word people." When the devil finds anyone who has made a commitment to live by faith, he knows that the only way he can deceive that person is by tricking him into thinking that what he is believing and living is the Word of God.

That's why we must always be on our guard against the subtlety, seduction and deceit of the one the Bible calls "the tempter." (Matt. 4:3.) The tempter is Satan, whom we are told to resist. Any temptation that is not resisted will lead to deception, and deception will result in sin, and sin will always produce tragic results: **But every man is tempted, when he is drawn away of his own lust, and enticed. Then when lust hath conceived, it bringeth forth sin: and sin, when it is finished, bringeth forth death** (James 1:14,15).

The Subtlety of Satan

And the woman said unto the serpent, We may eat of the fruit of the trees of the garden:

But of the fruit of the tree which is in the midst of the garden, God hath said, Ye shall not eat of it, neither shall ye touch it, lest ye die.

And the serpent said unto the woman, *Ye shall not surely die.*

For God doth know that in the day ye eat thereof, then your eyes shall be opened, and ye shall be as gods, knowing good and evil.

And when the woman saw that the tree was good for food, and that it was pleasant to the eyes, and a tree to be desired to make one wise, she took of the fruit thereof, and did eat, and gave also unto her husband with her; and he did eat.

And the eyes of them both were opened, and they knew that they were naked; and they sewed fig leaves together, and made themselves aprons.

And they heard the voice of the Lord God walking in the garden in the cool of the day: and Adam and his wife hid themselves from the presence of the Lord God amongst the trees of the garden.

Genesis 3:2-8

Notice the subtlety of Satan in this passage. He suggests to Eve that she should taste the fruit, assuring her that what God told her and her husband is not true, that they will not surely die because that's not what God really meant.

I don't believe that this was the first time that Eve had focused her attention on that tree, because James says that a person is tempted by being drawn away of his own lust. Eve must have passed that tree many times. It must have become an object of curiosity, even interest and appeal, to her. But she had probably resisted her feelings of fascination with it because of the Word of God which said, "Do not eat from this tree or you will surely die." But when the serpent came to her and she began to listen to him as he talked about the tree and how wonderful it was, she was soon persuaded to give in to her sinful desires.

This is what the psalmist was referring to when he said, **Blessed is the man that walketh not in the counsel of the ungodly, nor standeth in the way of sinners, nor sitteth in the seat of the scornful** (Ps. 1:1). In this verse we see three very distinct positions in regard to sin: "walk," "stand" and "sit."

You and I can walk by something enticing, but if we just keep on walking and don't stop, we may be able to stay out of trouble. For example, we can walk by pornography, and as long as we keep going, we're okay. But the moment we quit walking and start standing, that is an indication that it has grabbed our attention. Enticement has now become temptation. If we don't resist that temptation, our next step will be to sit — which naturally leads to sin.

That's why we have to learn to keep walking and

not pause to stand or sit in the presence of temptation of any kind. If we do, sooner or later we will end up compromising.

Charles Swindoll has defined the word *compromise* as "the erosion of our good intentions."[2] In this example, we walk by that enticing situation with the best of intentions to just keep going and not yield to temptation. But as soon as our attention is aroused and we stop walking, our good intentions have begun to erode. Once that erosion begins, it becomes harder and harder to find any ground on which to take a stand.

Notice that in the situation in the Garden of Eden, Satan told the woman, "You will not surely die. God knows that when you eat of this tree, your eyes will be opened and you will be as gods, knowing good and evil."

What was the woman's reaction? She looked at the tree and saw that it was "pleasant to the eyes." How long will it take for us to learn that not everything that is pleasant to our eyes is good for the rest of us?

The Bible speaks of the "lust of the eyes." (1 John 2:16.) Jesus said, **The light of the body is the eye: if therefore thine eye be single, thy whole body shall be full of light** (Matt. 6:22).

When it comes to faith, the two most important sense gates are the eyes and the ears, because what we see and what we hear goes directly down into our spirit.

---

[2]Charles R. Swindoll, *LIVING BEYOND THE DAILY GRIND: REFLECTIONS ON THE SONGS AND SAYINGS OF SCRIPTURE (BOOK 1)* (Dallas...London...Sydney...Singapore; Word, Canada, Richmond, B. C.: Word Publishing, 1988), p. 6.

The eyes and the ears are the primary entrances into the heart. Satan knows that fact. That's why he approached Eve through her sense of sight (seeing the tree) and hearing (listening to his voice).

Have you ever noticed that when you hear a certain catchy song or jingle several times, you will sometimes end up singing, whistling or humming it over and over for days? Even though it may be driving you crazy, you can't seem to get it out of your system. Why is that? Because it has got down into your spirit, and once that happens it's very hard to get it out.

That's why the Bible tells us not to walk in the counsel of the ungodly. That's why we need to stay away from whiners, complainers and defeatists, those who talk negativism, doubt and fear. Because what we listen to will get down into our spirit and will influence our attitude and actions.

In 1 Timothy 2:14 the Apostle Paul writes: **And Adam was not deceived, but the woman being deceived was in the transgression.** Because Eve allowed herself to be deceived by the serpent, because she listened to the devil and yielded to the lust of her eyes, she and her husband forfeited their heritage of faith and were no longer able to walk in the blessing of God.

By his subtlety, Satan was able to rob man and woman of their birthright of blessings and to interrupt God's planned lineage of faith in the earth.

The Stolen Blessing

And it came to pass, that when Isaac was old, and his eyes were dim, so that he could not see, he called Esau his

eldest son, and said unto him, My son: and he said unto him, Behold, here am I.

And he said, Behold now, I am old, I know not the day of my death:

Now therefore take, I pray thee, thy weapons, thy quiver and thy bow, and go out to the field, and take me some venison;

And make me savoury meat, such as I love, and bring it to me, that I may eat; that my soul may bless thee before I die.

And Rebekah heard when Isaac spake to Esau his son. And Esau went to the field to hunt for venison, and to bring it.

And Rebekah spake unto Jacob her son saying, Behold, I heard thy father speak unto Esau thy brother, saying,

Bring me venison, and make me savoury meat, that I may eat, and bless thee before the Lord before my death.

Now therefore, my son, obey my voice according to that which I command thee.

Go now to the flock, and fetch me from thence two good kids of the goats; and I will make them savoury meat for thy father, such as he loveth:

And thou shalt bring it to thy father, that he may eat, and that he may bless thee before his death.

And Jacob said to Rebekah his mother, Behold, Esau my brother is a hairy man, and I am a smooth man:

My father peradventure will feel me, and I shall seem to him as a deceiver; and I shall bring a curse upon me, and not a blessing.

And his mother said unto him, Upon me be thy curse, my son: only obey my voice, and go fetch me them.

And he went, and fetched, and brought them to his mother: and his mother made savoury meat, such as his father loved.

And Rebekah took goodly raiment of her eldest son Esau, which were with her in the house, and put them upon Jacob her younger son:

And she put the skins of the kids of the goats upon his hands, and upon the smooth of his neck:

And she gave the savoury meat and the bread, which she had prepared, into the hand of her son Jacob.

And he came unto his father, and said, My father: and he said, Here am I; who art thou, my son?

And Jacob said unto his father, I am Esau thy firstborn; I have done according as thou badest me: arise, I pray thee, sit and eat of my venison, that thy soul may bless me.

And Isaac said unto his son, How is it that thou hast found it so quickly, my son? And he said, Because the Lord thy God brought it to me.

And Isaac said unto Jacob, Come near, I pray thee, that I may feel thee, my son, whether thou be my very son Esau or not.

And Jacob went near unto Isaac his father; and he felt him, and said, The voice is Jacob's voice, but the hands are the hands of Esau.

And he discerned him not, because his hands were hairy, as his brother Esau's hands: so he blessed him.

And he said, Art thou my very son Esau? And he said, I am.

And he said, Bring it near to me, and I will eat of my son's venison, that my soul may bless thee. And he brought it near to him, and he did eat: and he brought him wine, and he drank.

And his father Isaac said unto him, Come near now, and kiss me, my son.

And he came near, and kissed him: and he smelled the smell of his raiment, and blessed him, and said, See, the smell of my son is as the smell of a field which the Lord hath blessed:

Therefore God give thee of the dew of heaven, and the fatness of the earth, and plenty of corn and wine:

Let people serve thee, and nations bow down to thee: be lord over thy brethren, and let thy mother's sons bow down to thee: cursed be every one that curseth thee, and blessed be he that blesseth thee.

Genesis 27:1-29

Whose blessing did Isaac bestow upon Jacob?

Esau's!

The blessing rightfully belonged to the elder son Esau, but through the blindness and gullibility of his father Isaac and the trickery and deceit of his mother Rebekah, Esau lost his blessing to his younger brother Jacob.

In Ephesians 1:3 the Apostle Paul tells us that God **...hath blessed us with all spiritual blessings in heavenly places in Christ.** Notice the tense of this sentence: "God hath blessed us with all spiritual blessings." We are not going to be blessed, or trying to be blessed; we are already blessed. If we are not walking in that blessing, it is because someone has stolen it from us, just as Jacob stole Esau's blessing. And there is a very strong possibility that our blessing was stolen from us through deception, just as Esau's was taken from him by deception.

The blessing of the father Isaac did not belong to Jacob. It belonged to Esau. However, a deceptive plan was devised whereby Jacob walked into the inheritance that rightfully belonged to his older brother.

According to the Bible, Satan should be under our feet. He has already been declared a defeated foe. Jesus has already stripped him of his power and of his armor and of his death-dealing blows. (Col. 2:14,15.) As the seed of Abraham, we are entitled to all the blessings of our spiritual father. (Gal. 3:13-29.) And one of the blessings that we should be enjoying is that of being the head and not the tail, above only and not beneath. (Deut. 28:13.)

Now, if you and I are not the head, if we are not above only, then we have been deceived. Someone has stolen our blessing.

One of the meanings of the word *bless* is "to speak well of."[3] God has already spoken well of us. (Eph. 1:3.) He has already declared that no weapon that is formed against us shall prosper. (Is. 54:17.) God has already declared that we are the head and not the tail, above only and not beneath; that we are blessed coming in and going out, in the city and in the country; that everything we put our hand to will prosper. (Deut. 28:1-13.) That is our blessing. If we are not enjoying all that, it is because we have been deceived and our blessing has been stolen from us. Someone else is enjoying what we should be enjoying — and that someone else is the deceiver, Satan.

The devil has to be subtle because he has no power whatsoever except that which he steals from the Church through deception.

Subtlety Steals Both
Birthright and Blessing

And it came to pass, as soon as Isaac had made an end of blessing Jacob, and Jacob was yet scarce gone out from

---

[3]James Strong, *Strong's Exhaustive Concordance of the Bible* (Nashville: Abingdon, 1890), "Greek Dictionary of the New Testament," p. 33, entry #2127.

the presence of Isaac his father, that Esau his brother came in from his hunting.

And he also had made savoury meat, and brought it unto his father, and said unto his father, Let my father arise, and eat of his son's venison, that thy soul may bless me.

And Isaac his father said unto him, Who art thou? And he said, I am thy son, thy firstborn Esau.

And Isaac trembled very exceedingly, and said, Who? where is he that hath taken venison, and brought it me, and I have eaten of all before thou camest, and have blessed him? yea, and he shall be blessed.

And when Esau heard the words of his father, he cried with a great and exceeding bitter cry, and said unto his father, Bless me, even me also, O my father.

And he said, *Thy brother came with subtlety, and hath taken away thy blessing.*

And he said, Is not he rightly named Jacob? for he hath supplanted me these two times: *he took away my birthright; and, behold, now he hath taken away my blessing....*

Genesis 27:30-36

Here we see illustrated the spiritual truth that the only way Satan can take away our blessing is through subtlety or subterfuge. That's why we have to be eternally vigilant, constantly alert, forever on our guard.

Esau said that not only had Jacob taken away his birthright, his heritage, but that he had also taken away his blessing. I can promise you that if we forfeit our heritage, as Esau did, the next thing we will lose will be our blessing.

If you and I let go of our heritage of faith, we are giving away our blessing. If, in our walk of faith, we cave in, give up and draw back under pressure, we are in essence conveying to the devil the title deed to everything that is rightfully ours. That's why we are told in Hebrews 10:35, **Cast not away therefore your confidence, which hath great recompence of reward.**

There is a reward, a blessing, for those who hold fast to their heritage. The only reward for those who draw back is the blessing of repentance. Thank God there is always the opportunity to repent and start all over again. But that is not God's best for His children. His best is for them to hold fast to their heritage of faith and not lose their blessing.

You Will Be Let Up When You Get Fed Up!

...And he said, Hast thou not reserved a blessing for me?

And Isaac answered and said unto Esau, Behold, I have made him thy lord, and all his brethren have I given to him for servants; and with corn and wine have I sustained him: and what shall I do now unto thee, my son?

And Esau said unto his father, Hast thou but one blessing, my father? bless me, even me also, O my father. And Esau lifted up his voice, and wept.

And Isaac his father answered and said unto him. Behold, thy dwelling shall be the fatness of the earth, and of the dew of heaven from above;

And by thy sword shalt thou live, and shalt serve thy brother; and *it shall come to pass when thou shalt have the dominion, that thou shalt break his yoke from off thy neck.*

Genesis 27:36-40

Isaac is saying to Esau, "Because your heritage and your blessing have been stolen from you, your way is not going to be an easy one. You are going to have to live by your sword and serve your brother. But if you won't give up, there will come a time when you will regain the dominion in which you should be rightfully walking. You will break his yoke off your neck and once again be free."

To get the full impact of what Isaac is telling Esau in this passage, let's examine it in two other translations. The *New International Version* of Genesis 27:39,40 says:

> **His father Isaac answered him,**
> **"Your dwelling will be**
> **away from the earth's richness,**
> **away from the dew of heaven**
> **above.**
> **You will live by the sword**
> **and you will serve your brother.**
> **But *when you grow restless*,**
> **you will throw his yoke**
> **from off your neck."**

What does that phrase **when you grow restless** mean? Let me put it into Texas terms: "When you get *fed up!*"

When you and I get "fed up," when we get to the point that we will not take any more of the devil's robbing us of what rightfully belongs to us, then we will throw his yoke off our neck!

You see, we never get the devil off our back until we grow restless in the Spirit — until we get fed up with being deceived, fed up with being the tail and not the head, fed up with being beneath and not above, fed up with never being blessed but always living under a curse.

What happens in our world when people get fed up with some unfair situation? They take action. When people get fed up with living in political subjugation, they rise up to overthrow their oppressors. When people get fed up with being held in economic bondage, they revolt against those who are dishonestly depriving them of the good things of this life. In our generation we have seen this kind of thing happening all around the globe, especially in the Eastern Bloc nations. When a wrong situation becomes unbearable, people rise up and do something about it. You and I can walk around all of our life talking about how bad we have it, about how we never had a chance, about how we were brought up on the wrong side of the tracks, about how we were never allowed the freedoms and opportunities others enjoyed. We can make all of the excuses known to mankind to explain why our life is like it is. But our situation will never change until we get fed up with it and decide to quit whining and complaining and start doing something about it.

The only reason we are Christians today is because we got fed up with being unbelievers. We walk in the blessing of salvation today because at some time in the past we did something about our miserable lost condition. In the same way, we will begin to walk in divine health when we get so fed up with being sick that we do something about it. We will begin to walk in financial prosperity when we get so fed up with being poor that we take action. We will begin to walk in the blessing of Abraham when we get so fed up with living under a curse that we rise up against Satan and break his yoke from off our neck.

The Living Bible paraphrase of Genesis 27:39,40 reads:

Isaac: "Yours will be no life of ease and
luxury, but you shall hew your way
with your sword. *For a time you will
serve your brother, but you will finally
shake loose from him and be free.*"

For a time now you and I may have been living a
lower lifestyle than God intended for us, but when we
get spiritually fed up, we will shake loose from the devil
and break his yoke from off our neck!

Notice that this version says that we will have to
hew our way with our sword. In Ephesians 6:17 we are
told to take the sword of the Spirit, which is the Word of
God. Why? So we can use it to hew our way through to
victory over the one who has stolen our blessing.

That too is a part of our precious heritage of faith!

7

Waging Spiritual Warfare

> When thou goest out to battle against thine enemies, and seest horses, and chariots, and a people more than thou, be not afraid of them: *for the Lord thy God is with thee*, which brought thee up out of the land of Egypt.
>
> And it shall be, when ye are come nigh unto the battle, that the priest shall approach and speak unto the people,
>
> And shall say unto them, Hear, O Israel, ye approach this day unto battle against your enemies: let not your hearts faint, fear not, and do not tremble, neither be ye terrified because of them;
>
> For the Lord your God is he that goeth with you, to fight for you against your enemies, to save you.
>
> Deuteronomy 20:1-4

Jude tells us that we are to **...earnestly contend for the faith which was once delivered unto the saints** (Jude 3). The word *contend* means to fight.[1]

As Christians we are to be engaged in spiritual warfare. We do not fight against other people, against those who do not share our faith, but at the same time we don't let them talk us out of our faith and lose our blessing. Instead, we put on the full armor of God, take

---

[1]James Strong, *Strong's Exhaustive Concordance of the Bible* (Nashville: Abingdon, 1890), "Greek Dictionary of the Bible," p. 30, entry #1864, from p. 8, entry #75, "fight, labor fervently, strive."

up the shield of faith and wield the sword of the Spirit, which is the Word of God, as we launch into attack against our spiritual enemies.

In speaking of warfare, we are reminded of the warning we received in Psalm 78 about the children of Ephraim who, **...being armed, and carrying bows, turned back in the day of battle** (v. 9). The psalmist called them **...a stubborn and rebellious generation; a generation that set not their heart aright, and whose spirit was not stedfast with God** (v. 8).

Here in this passage from Deuteronomy 20 we are being told, "Don't be like those people. When you take the sword and begin to hew your way through, you must not throw down your weapons and run away as they did."

When you and I go into battle, the worst thing we can do is to lay down our weapons. When we come under pressure or attack from the enemy, the last thing we want to do is to drop the sword of Spirit, which is the Word of God. Without it, we have nothing to fight with. The shield of faith is designed as a defensive weapon. Its purpose is "to quench every fiery dart of the wicked one." (Eph. 6:16.) The sword of the Spirit, on the other hand, is an offensive weapon. Its purpose is to attack the enemy.

The Lord tells us in this passage that when we face the enemy, who may appear to be more numerous and more powerful than we are, we must not be intimidated. Even though the situation may look impossible, even though in the natural it may seem that there is absolutely no way we can possibly win, we must not faint or be afraid. Why not? Because the Lord our God goes with us to fight against our enemies.

As long as we have the sword of the Spirit, the Word of God, and are engaged in aggressive spiritual warfare, we can be assured of one thing: God is on our side. He is warring right alongside us. And not only has He promised to fight with us and for us, He has also promised to save and deliver us, to cause us to be victorious over all the power of the enemy. (Luke 10:19.)

The key to success in spiritual warfare is *attitude*. We must take a stand of faith and not panic in the midst of adversity.

No matter how the situation may look to us, we must not be terrified. Regardless of the size or ferocity of the enemy, we must not allow ourselves to be overcome by doubt or fear. We must not drop our weapons and give up the fight. Instead we must stand our ground, and having done all, to stand. (Eph. 6:13.) We must be skilled, courageous warriors — like David and his mighty men.

Mighty Men of War

These be the names of the mighty men whom David had: The Tachmonite that sat in the seat, chief among the captains; the same was Adino the Eznite: *he lift up his spear against eight hundred, whom he slew at one time.*

And after him was Eleazar the son of Dodo the Ahohite, one of the three mighty men with David, when they defied the Philistines that were there gathered together to battle, and the men of Israel were gone away:

He arose, and smote the Philistines until his hand was weary, and his hand clave unto the sword: and the Lord wrought a great victory that day; and the people returned after him only to spoil.

And after him was Shammah the son of Agee the Hararite. And the Philistines were gathered together into a troop, where was a piece of ground full of lentiles: and the people fled from the Philistines.

But *he stood in the midst of the ground, and defended it, and slew the Philistines: and the Lord wrought a great victory.*

2 Samuel 23:8-12

Notice these three great men of war. The first slew eight hundred of the dreaded Philistines singlehandedly. The second stood his ground and fought until he was exhausted, until he thought he couldn't stand a minute longer. Yet he was so determined to hold on to what was rightfully his that when the battle was over, his hand had to be pried from his sword.

That's the attitude we should have toward our heritage of faith. We should be so determined to preserve our precious heritage and to keep our wonderful blessing that we absolutely refuse to let go or back down. We should go on "holding faith" so firmly that when the battle is over, our hand will have to be pried away from the sword of the Spirit.

Finally, there was Shammah, who took his stand in a field of lentils and refused to budge. He made up his mind that that little patch of earth belonged to him, and he was not about to give it up. He stood alone in the middle of that field and boldly declared, "No enemy is going to take what is rightfully mine." He stood his ground and fought off an entire troop of soldiers by himself so that when the other Israelites returned to the scene, there was nothing left but the spoils of battle. Because of this one man's great courage and determination, the Lord won a great victory through him.

Now let me ask you something: How determined are you to hold on to what is rightfully yours? How determined are you to preserve your heritage of faith? How determined are you to keep and enjoy the blessings that have been purchased for you by the shed blood of the Lord Jesus Christ?

Satan is trying to steal your birthright and rob you of your blessing. Are you going to stand by and let him get away with it? Or are you going to fight for what is rightfully yours? The devil may be trying to steal your health, your job, your finances, your marriage, your peace of mind and heart, your spouse or your children. Whatever he is out to steal from you, you must take your sword in hand and boldly declare, "Satan, get away from me!" The Bible says that if you will do that, he will flee from you.

David's mighty men knew how to take a stand and not be moved from it. They were determined warriors who would not cast away their confidence. They fought until they had no strength to fight anymore — then they straightened up and fought some more. They drew a line of faith on the ground and refused to step back from it. And when the battle was all over, everyone saw that God had given them a great victory.

That is what you and I are to do. But in order to do that, we must remember what we are told in Deuteronomy 20:3. We must not be afraid of our enemy or terrified by him. We must not allow ourselves to become weary to the point of giving up. If we do, if we cave in and draw back, we will not reap the reward of our faith — which the Lord had promised *will* be ours in due season, if we faint not.

In "Due Season"

**And let us not be weary in well doing: for *in due*
season we shall reap, if we faint not.**

Galatians 6:9

It is true that in this context the Apostle Paul is
talking about sowing and reaping. However, the
principle is the same whether applied to sowing and
reaping, walking in faith or waging spiritual warfare. If
we do not allow ourselves to become weary to the point
of giving up, we will reap the reward of our patience
and efforts. If we will be faithful and obedient,
eventually the manifestation of our faith will come.

God doesn't say, "If you sow, you *may* reap." Instead,
He says, "If you sow, you *will* reap." When God speaks
of the manifestation of His Word, He never says "*if* it
comes to pass," He always says "*when* it comes to pass."
With God, the full manifestation is always just a matter
of time — or a matter of *timing*. His Word always
manifests "in due season."

You and I may not know when "due season" will
arrive, but we can be assured that it is coming, because
God has said so in His Word, and God is not a man that
He should lie. (Num. 23:19.)

How long do we have to stand in faith for the
manifestation of God's Word?

Until "due season" comes.

How long will that be?

Until we don't have to stand any longer.

What I mean is that we must stand until the
manifestation comes; once that happens, then we don't
have to stand anymore.

It's just that simple.

You will always know when "due season" has arrived, because you will see the manifestation and will no longer have to stand in faith for it.

Has the money you have been standing in faith for manifested yet? Has the healing that you have been standing in faith for manifested yet? Has the answer to the problem that you have been standing in faith for manifested yet? If not, then you must go on standing a while longer until it does manifest.

You may never know when it is *going* to manifest if you go on standing, but you can always know that it will *never* manifest if you give up and quit standing.

"Due season" always arrives, but only for those who are waiting in earnest expectation of it, those who refuse to give in under pressure, those who refuse to panic in the face of the enemy.

Since you never know when "due season" is going to arrive, and since it is your responsibility to stand in faith for it, then why not act as though it could happen at any moment?

"Oh, but I wouldn't want to get my hopes up."

That's why you don't have any "due seasons." I get my hopes up all the time. In fact, I keep them up. I am expectant. If the manifestation doesn't come today, then I expect it tomorrow. If it doesn't come tomorrow, then I expect it the next day.

Wouldn't it be sad to stand in faith for six months and then get weary and faint and give up — only to learn that had you stood in faith one more day the manifestation would have come? Doesn't that motivate you to want to keep on standing? What have you got to lose? If nothing is working for you by not standing, then why not try standing? You have nothing to lose by standing and waiting for the arrival of "due season" and everything to lose if you don't. So keep standing, because with God it's not *if* it happens, but *when* it happens.

With the Lord, there is a "due season" for everything. The manifestation may not be instantaneous, but it is always well worth waiting for.

Don't Panic!

And when Jesus was passed over again by ship unto the other side, much people gathered unto him: and he was nigh unto the sea.

And, behold, there cometh one of the rulers of the synagogue, Jairus by name; and when he saw him, he fell at his feet,

And besought him greatly, saying, My little daughter lieth at the point of death: I pray thee, come and lay thy hands on her, that she may be healed; and she shall live.

And Jesus went with him; and much people followed him, and thronged him.

And a certain woman, which had an issue of blood twelve years,

And had suffered many things of many physicians, and had spent all that she had, and was nothing bettered, but rather grew worse,

When she had heard of Jesus, came in the press behind, and touched his garment.

For she said, If I may touch but his clothes, I shall be whole.

And straightway the fountain of her blood was dried up; and she felt in her body that she was healed of that plague.

And Jesus, immediately knowing in himself that virtue had gone out of him, turned him about in the press, and said, Who touched my clothes?

And his disciples said unto him, Thou seest the multitude thronging thee, and sayest thou, Who touched me?

And he looked round about to see her that had done this thing.

But the woman fearing and trembling, knowing what was done in her, came and fell down before him, and told him all the truth.

And he said unto her, Daughter, thy faith hath made thee whole; go in peace, and be whole of thy plague.

While he yet spake, there came from the ruler of the synagogue's house certain which said, Thy daughter is dead: why troublest thou the Master any further?

As soon as Jesus heard the word that was spoken, he saith unto the ruler of the synagogue, *Be not afraid, only believe.*

Mark 5:21-36

Notice that as soon as Jairus, the religious leader whose daughter was dying, spoke his faith, Jesus was attracted by that faith and went with him to heal her. As He and Jairus and the disciples were making their way through the multitude thronging Him, a woman came up behind Him and secretly touched the hem of His garment. This was a touch of faith.

Jesus turned and asked, "Who touched Me?"

His disciples said to Him, "Lord, You see this huge crowd that is pressing against You on all sides, so how can You ask who touched You? Everyone is touching You!"

But Jesus said, "This touch was different, because I felt virtue go out of Me."

I like to paraphrase it by saying, "Someone has made a demand upon My ability."

Now put yourself in Jairus' place. Here he has desperately made his way through the crowds to Jesus to beg Him to come and heal his daughter who is at death's door. Obviously, he wants Jesus to hurry up and come as quickly as possible because there is not a moment to lose.

But then on the way, some woman sneaks up behind Jesus and by an act of faith makes a demand upon His ability. As Jesus stops to minister to her, Jairus is left standing there to watch the scene and think within himself: "This isn't fair. This woman has been sick for twelve years, but my daughter is dying right now. I came to Jesus first. He should come with me and heal my daughter, then He can attend to this woman. Besides, since she is unclean, she doesn't even have a right to be here."

The Levitical law stated that because this woman had an issue of blood, she was ceremonially unclean. By law, she could have been stoned to death just for going out in public. Here Jesus was taking up precious time with this social outcast when it seemed that He should have been dealing with the daughter of the ruler of the synagogue.

This is evidence that Jesus is no respecter of persons.

(Acts 10:34.) He will minister to the highest-ranking people in society, and He will minister to the lowest outcasts of society. He had started going along with Jairus in response to his faith, and on the way He stopped and ministered to this poor woman in response to her faith. This demonstrates the fact that the Lord is not looking for those who have wealth, position or power, all He is looking for is someone with faith. Faith always gets His full and undivided attention.

As Jesus is talking with the woman, messengers come from Jairus' house to tell him that his daughter has died, so there is no reason to "trouble" the Master any further. The use of this word *trouble* gives me the impression that perhaps Jairus was saying to Jesus, "Master, please hurry! We've got to get back to my house right away! Let this woman go so we can get out of here!"

Notice that Jesus heard what the messengers told Jairus about his daughter being dead. Immediately He turned to Jairus and said to him, **Be not afraid; only believe.** In other words, "Don't panic!" By so doing, He was telling this man to act just as he had been acting before he received this bad report.

One paraphrase of this passage reads as follows:

> **Gently Jesus said to her, "Your trust has made you whole, daughter. Go your way in peace, and continue to be well." While he was talking with her, messengers from the official's house arrived and said to Jairus, "Your daughter is dead; don't bother the teacher any longer." When Jesus heard the report, he said to Jairus, "Do not panic. Only trust."[2]**

---

[2]Ben Campbell Johnson, *Matthew and Mark: A Relational Paraphrase* (Waco: Word Books, 1978), p. 120.

As far as Jesus was concerned, death was no greater challenge than sickness. He knew that if He had the power to restore health, He had the power to restore life. That's why He told Jairus not to panic.

Panic Defined

Let me give you a dictionary definition of the word *panic*: "a sudden, unreasonable, overpowering fear."[3]

Since panic is unreasonable fear, it is groundless fear, which means that there is no factual evidence to support or substantiate it. I like to put it this way: panic is a smoke screen.

The devil loves to throw up a smoke screen to cause us to fear, because he knows that we have been taught all our lives that where there is smoke, there is fire. This is what we call in Texas "making a mountain out of a molehill." Texans are often accused of exaggerating, especially when talking about their state. But Satan is the master exaggerator. He exaggerates everything. He blows things up all out of proportion. That's how he gets people to let go of their faith and give in to panic.

If you are in panic, then you are operating in groundless fear, and fear of any kind negates faith. Faith and fear are mutually exclusive. They cannot exist at the same time in the same person.

Either you have great faith or you have great fear, one or the other. Satan knows that if he can drive your faith out of you by fear, he can bring to pass in your life the very thing that you are fearing. But if you keep faith

---

[3]*Funk and Wagnalls New Comprehensive International Dictionary of the English Language,* s.v. "panic."

in your mind and heart, God will bring to pass in your life the very thing that you are believing.

That's why Jesus told Jairus, "Don't be afraid. Only believe." Obviously Jairus' mental and emotional attitude had a great deal to do with what was going to happen next.

The same is true with us.

When the Lord tells us not to be afraid, not to panic, He is not saying that the negative situations we are facing are not real. They are real, just as this man's situation was real. Jairus' daughter was dead. That is about as real as it gets. Jesus did not deny the reality of the situation, but He did indicate by His words and actions that it was not the *ultimate* or *final* reality. He went right on toward Jairus' house just as He had been doing before the bad report came. He had started out with Jairus in response to his faith, and He didn't intend to stop now just because the physical circumstances had changed.

Jesus didn't tell this man, "Too bad, Jairus. If I hadn't got stopped by this woman, we might have made it in time. It must not have been the will of God that your daughter be healed. If it had been His will, she would have lasted until we arrived on the scene. I'm sorry, but it's just too late for Me to do anything now, so I may as well go My way."

That's not what Jesus said, and it's not what He did. He went right on toward Jairus' house just as if nothing had happened.

When Jesus starts walking toward your house, He doesn't care what storms arise along the way. As far as

He is concerned, He is going to continue in your direction until you get your miracle — *if* you won't let go of your faith!

Faith Attracts the Lord

The thing that attracts Jesus is faith. Faith is what draws Him. If you will hold onto your faith, then you will keep Jesus' attention. He is always looking for faith. As we have seen, that is what He will be looking for when He returns to the earth, and that is what He is looking for in the meantime. That is what He was looking for when He was here in the flesh.

Do you remember the story about the time Jesus was preaching in a house that was so full no one else could get in? The Bible says that at that time the power of the Lord was present to heal. (Luke 5:17.) Yet not a soul in that overcrowded building was being healed. Not until four men brought their friend who had the palsy, carried him up onto the roof of the house, tore off the tiles and lowered him down through the ceiling on a pallet right in front of Jesus. The Bible says, **When he saw their faith...**(Luke 5:20), He healed the man.

Jesus is always looking for faith. Wherever there is faith, that's where He will be found. If He finds faith in you, He will head toward your house, just as He did with Jairus. It doesn't make any difference what happens between the moment that He leaves and the time He arrives. If He intends to bring you a miracle, and if He keeps finding faith in you, then you will get that miracle — regardless of the circumstances!

Jesus is not moved by outward appearances, only by inward faith. That's why He told Jairus, "Don't panic. Keep believing."

No matter what you hear, no matter how severe the report, no matter how bad things may look on the outside, don't panic. Don't take your eyes off Jesus or your faith off the line. Don't drop your weapons and flee. Stand your ground and defend your field. Take that sword of the Spirit, which is the Word of God, and make up your mind that, come what may, you are going to hold on to what is rightfully yours. Don't let a bad report cause you to doubt and fear. Don't let Satan rob you of your precious heritage of faith and the blessing of Abraham that rightfully belongs to you.

Don't Let Go of Your Faith!

And *he suffered no man to follow him, save Peter, and James, and John the brother of James.*

And he cometh to the house of the ruler of the synagogue, and seeth the tumult, and them that wept and wailed greatly.

And when he was come in, he saith unto them, Why make ye this ado, and weep? the damsel is not dead, but sleepeth.

And they laughed him to scorn. *But when he had put them all out, he taketh the father and the mother of the damsel, and them that were with him, and entereth in where the damsel was lying.*

And he took the damsel by the hand, and saith unto her, Talitha cumi; which is, being interpreted, *Damsel, I say unto thee, arise.*

And straightway the damsel arose, and walked; for she was of the age of twelve years. And they were astonished with a great astonishment.

Mark 5:37-42

Here we see the end of the story about Jairus' daughter. Jesus walked into his house, took her by the hand and said, "Little girl, I say unto you, arise." And she did!

I want you to know that if you won't let go of your faith, Jesus can not only resurrect your daughter or your son or your spouse, He can resurrect your physical body, your marriage, your finances, anything that the world says is dead. It may *be* dead, but when Jesus arrives on the scene, so does resurrection power!

When Jesus set out for the home of Jairus, why did He take with Him only Peter, James and John? Once there, why did He put out everyone from the room but these disciples and the mother and father of the girl? Because He wanted around Him only those who had faith.

Jesus is looking for faith. Will he find it in you?

Be Not Afraid

And straightway Jesus constrained his disciples to get into a ship, and to go before him unto the other side, while he sent the multitudes away.

And when he had sent the multitudes away, he went up into a mountain apart to pray: and when the evening was come, he was there alone.

But the ship was now in the midst of the sea, tossed with waves: for the wind was contrary.

And in the fourth watch of the night Jesus went unto them, walking on the sea.

And when the disciples saw him walking on the sea, they were troubled, saying, It is a spirit; and they cried out for fear.

But straightway Jesus spake unto them, saying, *Be of good cheer; it is I; be not afraid.*

And Peter answered him and said, Lord, if it be thou, bid me come unto thee on the water.

And he said, Come. And when Peter was come down out of the ship, he walked on the water, to go to Jesus.

But when he saw the wind boisterous, he was afraid; and beginning to sink, he cried, saying, Lord, save me.

And immediately Jesus stretched forth his hand, and caught him, and said unto him, *O thou of little faith, wherefore didst thou doubt?*

And when they were come into the ship, *the wind ceased.*

Then they that were in the ship came and worshipped him, saying, Of a truth thou art the Son of God.

Matthew 14:22-33

Let's get a picture of what is happening here in this scene. In the middle of a stormy night on a raging sea, Jesus suddenly appears out of the darkness and begins moving toward His disciples, walking on the churning waters. Thinking He is a ghost, the men are frightened out of their wits. In that perilous situation, it seems to them that death is inevitable.

Realizing that His unexpected and unexplained appearance has frightened them, Jesus shouts to them, "Calm down; it's Me. Don't panic!"

Although they recognize His voice, they are still having a hard time believing that it is their Master, so Peter yells, "Lord, if it's really You out there, order me to come to You on the water."

"Come," answers Jesus.

So Peter steps down out of the ship and begins to walk toward Jesus on the water.

That took courage on Peter's part.

Remember, all this is taking place in the dark of night on a raging sea, with the wind howling and the waves billowing up all around. Yet in the midst of that outward tumult, and in spite of his own inward upheaval, Peter responds to one single word from the Lord — "Come."

Not only did that take courage, it took faith.

The boat is rocking back and forth, the waves are being tossed to and fro, and everyone around him is scared and confused, yet this man has the audacity to step out of that heaving, battered little ship and set out to walk on the rolling sea. Although Peter is as frightened as the others, that one word "Come" from the Lord strengthens and encourages him enough that he can overcome his fear and step out in faith.

Now many people have the mistaken idea that the moment Peter stepped out of that little ship, he began to sink. That's not so. He walked on the water to Jesus. Evidently he got pretty close to Him because when he did give in to fear and begin to sink and cry out for help, Jesus was able simply to reach out His hand and lift him up out of the angry sea.

Although he was successful for a time, Peter began to sink, "when he saw the wind boisterous." In other words, when he took his eyes off Jesus and began to look at what was going on around him, Peter got scared and started to go under.

This is a beautiful example of panic, of groundless fear.

What do you think was going through Peter's mind when he saw "the wind boisterous"? He was supernaturally walking on the sea, so the only thing that could have caused him to fail was the thought, "Peter, you fool, you know you can't walk on water when it's windy!"

That's the only thing his mind could have told him, because the wind was blowing before Jesus appeared. It was blowing when Peter stepped out of the boat. It was blowing all the time he was walking toward Jesus on the water. The wind was there all the while. But it was only when Peter took his eyes off of His Savior and focused his attention on the wind that he began to sink.

What happened? Peter allowed himself to be panicked by a smoke screen. He gave into groundless fear — and without any ground on which to stand, naturally he began to sink.

So Peter cried out to Jesus, "Save me, Lord!" Jesus reached out His hand, grabbed him and said to him, "O you of little faith, why did you doubt?"

Jesus wasn't reprimanding Peter for being so foolish as to think that he could walk on water. After all, He was the One Who had called Peter to do that very thing. Jesus was rebuking Peter for giving in to fear and doubt and allowing his faith to be stolen from him.

Hold Faith — and Then Pass It On!

Notice what happened when Jesus and Peter got back into the ship: "the wind ceased." Now Jesus didn't rebuke the wind and tell it to be still as He did in Mark 4:39. Why not? Because the wind was not a problem in this case; it was just a smoke screen — it was about to stop anyway.

Do you realize what this means? It means that the devil tries his best to cause us to panic just when our problem is about to resolve itself. You can always count on it. When the pressure becomes the greatest, that is a sign that the wind is about to cease. The devil is desperately hoping you will cave in and draw back before the storm lets up and you sail into still waters.

Any time Satan tells you that your situation is hopeless, that there is no way out, you can be sure he has just got the news that the wind is about to cease and the storm is about to blow itself out. That's why he is so desperate to cause you to panic, to give up your faith — and sink.

The things that cause us to panic, give up our faith and sink are always temporary. Tests, trials and temptations are all seasonal. So are opposition and adversity. Nothing lasts forever. This too will pass. As powerful and menacing as the storm may be, it will eventually move on. If you and I will stand firm and resist the devil, if we will refuse to panic, the storm will blow over, and the wind will cease.

"Due season" is on its way! You are going to reap your reward, if you faint not. Don't panic. Don't give in to groundless fear. Take your stand and keep on "holding faith" — your precious heritage — and then pass it on!

Conclusion:
A Legacy of Faith

Don't ever forget those wonderful days when you first learned about Christ. Remember how you kept right on with the Lord even though it meant terrible suffering. Sometimes you were laughed at and beaten, and sometimes you watched and sympathized with others suffering the same things. You suffered with those thrown into jail, and you were actually joyful when all you owned was taken from you, knowing that better things were awaiting you in heaven, things that would be yours forever.

Do not let this happy trust in the Lord die away, no matter what happens. Remember your reward! You need to keep on patiently doing God's will if you want him to do for you all that he has promised. His coming will not be delayed much longer.

And those whose faith has made them good in God's sight must live by faith, trusting him in everything. Otherwise, if they shrink back, God will have no pleasure in them.

But we have never turned our backs on God and sealed our fate. No, our faith in him assures our souls' salvation.

Hebrews 10:32-39 TLB

In this study we have seen that God is interested in *longevity*. He is looking for people who will stick with Him through thick and thin, come what may. He is looking for people who are not satisfied with a temporary experience, but who want a lifetime relationship of faith and trust — those who will then pass that lifestyle on to their children and grandchildren and succeeding generations.

Some people are faithful to the Lord and His Word as long as everything is going well. But as soon as things turn against them, they give up and quit.

You and I live in a society of quitters. If you don't believe me, just look at our divorce rate. Each year thousands of couples vow to love and cherish and honor one another "till death do us part," and then turn around and split up at the first sign of trouble. That same attitude has become prevalent in the Body of Christ. Unless something happens to change this situation, those who follow after us will be a generation of quitters.

That's why it is so important that you and I "hold faith," that we not let "this happy trust in the Lord" die with us. That's why it is vital that no matter what happens, we "keep on patiently doing the will of God if we want Him to do all that He has promised." We cannot quit doing God's will, quit living by faith, quit acting on the Word of God, and still expect Him to fulfill His promises to us.

The Lord has said that His coming will not be delayed much longer. That's why we must not be among those who cave in and draw back and lose our reward, but among those who remain faithful and reap "in due season."

Not only must we keep on doing the will of God in order to receive our reward, not only must we "hold faith," but we must leave behind us a perpetual legacy of faith. Rather than being like Noah, who accomplished a great act of faith but failed to pass on his faith to his posterity, we must be like Abraham, "the father of faith," who taught his children and grandchildren to believe, cleave to, trust in and rely on the Word of God. (Heb. 10:39 AMP.) It is not enough for us to *demonstrate* faith, we must also *perpetuate* faith. Otherwise, our faith will die with us. And that is not God's plan or desire.

When God deals with man, He is more interested in lifestyle than experience. That's why He established an everlasting covenant with Adam, with Noah, with Abraham, with Jacob, with the children of Israel, and later with the Body of Christ. Why? So that He could create a lineage of faith that would continue until the return of His Son to this earth.

Before I went into the ministry, I was an automobile body repairman, like my father before me. My dad was an expert at his profession. As a child I would sit for hours and watch him at his job. He was a specialist, a perfectionist who took great pains with his work and great pride in his product. He used to tell me, "Son, whatever you choose to do in life, learn to do it right. Don't take shortcuts."

For many reasons, things have changed. Today there is little pride in work. The zeal for excellence has all but disappeared. Quality is a thing of the past. The art of true craftsmanship has virtually been lost because it has not been preserved and passed down from one generation to the next.

That is exactly what has happened in the life of faith. But God is holding you and me responsible for preserving and passing on to our children and grandchildren the precious art of living by faith. He expects succeeding generations to be even better at it than we are. That's why our lives must be an example of faith to others, so they can learn and follow the lifestyle of faith, and then pass it on to those who come after them.

The Legacy of Faith

Now faith is the substance of things hoped for, the evidence of things not seen.

For by it the elders obtained a good report.

Hebrews 11:1,2

The theme of the entire eleventh chapter of the book of Hebrews is *perpetual* faith. It begins with creation and comes down through the ages tracing the lineage of faith from one person and one generation to the next. Each verse begins with the phrase **By faith.... — By faith Enoch..., By faith Noah..., By faith Abraham...** and so on down the line through Isaac and Jacob and Joseph and Moses until verse 39 which states: **And these all...obtained a good report through faith....**

Then in the first verse of Chapter 12, we are told: **Wherefore seeing we also are compassed about with so great a cloud of witnesses, let us lay aside every weight, and the sin which doth so easily beset us, and let us run with patience the race that is set before us.**

What is the writer of Hebrews saying to us in this passage? He is saying that God has set before us a heritage of faith, one that has been passed down from person to person and generation to generation. All these people are gathered in heaven where they make up "a great cloud of witnesses" who are watching us and cheering us on. You and I have our own personal cheerleading section who is continually crying out to us: "You can do it! We did it, and so can you! Keep the faith! Remember your heritage! Pass it on!"

I don't know about you, but I will be very disappointed if my children and grandchildren do not live by the faith that I have modeled before them all my life. But I don't believe that is going to happen. I believe they *are* going to live by faith. Why? Because it is their family heritage.

The Seed of Abraham, the Father of Faith

Neither, because they are the seed of Abraham, are they all children: but, In Isaac shall thy seed be called.

That is, They which are the children of the flesh, these are not the children of God: but *the children of the promise are counted for the seed.*

Romans 9:7,8

I have said that my spiritual heritage runs from Abraham, through Isaac and Jacob, and from there down through time to Kenneth Hagin, Oral Roberts, Kenneth Copeland and me. Abraham, who is described as the father of faith, set in motion a new life of faith, one that has been passed down through the ages to you and me.

The Apostle Paul says that Abraham **...staggered not at the promise of God through unbelief; but was strong in faith, giving glory to God....being fully persuaded that, what he had promised, he was able also to perform** (Rom. 4:20,21). However, it is important to understand that Abraham was only a man, just as you and I are. Like us, he had to deal with doubt and unbelief. He too had to resist the temptation to "lean on the arm of flesh."

Although God had promised Abraham that he would father a child through whom would come whole nations, since Abraham was an old man and his wife Sarah was past the age of child-bearing, that seemed impossible in the natural. After some time had gone by and there was no such child, Abraham's wife Sarah came up with a bright idea. She talked Abraham into having a child by her handmaid Hagar. This son was named Ishmael.

This was not God's plan and was not pleasing to Him. If you read your Bible you will see that it was thirteen years after the birth of Ishmael before God even talked to Abraham again. Later Sarah did give birth to a son named Isaac, and there was constant trouble between Ishmael, the child of flesh, and Isaac, the child of promise.

The Ishmaels in our life can get us into trouble. Ishmaels are all those things that we produce in the flesh; Isaacs are all those things that are born of faith. It should be reassuring to us that even Abraham gave into doubt at least one time in his life. If he had never doubted, if he had never wavered, then he would not be a good example to us of one who *learned* to walk in faith — because we are not perfect either.

The life of Abraham reveals to us a man who was like us in every way. He had every opportunity to compromise, to stagger at the Word of God, just as we do. Yet there came a time when Abraham ceased to stagger and became strong in faith. He was no longer moved by what he saw, but instead he held firm to the

Word of God. He became a man of faith, and then passed on that faith to those who came after him. From that man, God established a legacy of faith which He expects us, as children of the promise, to carry on in our lives and to perpetuate in our families.

Faith Takes Time and Effort

The state of Texas is known for its Western wear. For generations some people there have made an art of producing hand-made cowboy boots. These are the finest quality boots money can buy — and the price shows it! When you go in to get a pair of these boots, you don't just sit down and pick them off the rack. The bootmaker takes careful measurements and then designs a pair of boots to fit you and nobody else. It may take him weeks to make them, but when he is finished, they will fit you like a glove.

Sadly, in our society today, many of the things we once appreciated as fine workmanship have been lost. The reason is because this generation doesn't want to put in the time and effort it takes to learn such a craft. Instead, we live in a high-tech society that demands instant gratification — fast food being a prime example.

I remember growing up in an era when quality time around the family table was precious and carefully guarded. Meal time was when family business was conducted. No one ran in and out or snatched a bite on the run. Everyone sat down together and took turns talking and listening to one another. Today, no one, it seems, has time for that anymore.

Also in my younger days, certain people in the family were famous for particular items they produced well. A grandmother might have a reputation for a special food she prepared. The young women wanted to spend time with her to learn from her the secrets of creating that tasty dish. This generation doesn't have either the time nor the inclination to do that.

And we are the poorer for it.

The same kind of thing has happened in the spiritual realm. Today, the pioneer trails seem to have all been blazed. The going has been made so smooth by now that much of the challenge has been eliminated. People have lost their spiritual tenacity.

Faith that comes too easily also goes just as easily.

Often people new to the faith do not appreciate what they have. They are not aware of the hardships and sacrifices of those who stood the test of time and adversity to see that they received the message and the precious inheritance of faith.

Success Requires a Successor

And when Abram was ninety years old and nine, the Lord appeared to Abram, and said unto him, I am the Almighty God; walk before me, and be thou perfect....

And I will establish my covenant between me and thee *and thy seed after thee* in their generations for an everlasting covenant, to be a God unto thee, and *to thy seed after thee*.

Genesis 17:1,7

It is displeasing to God when this great heritage of faith is not passed on. God wants this lifestyle of faith to be successive; in other words, to be passed down from one generation to the next.

I once heard Lester Sumrall say, "Success without a successor is failure." Brother Sumrall, a senior statesman of the faith, has preached on nearly every continent of the globe. His ministry has gone on for decades and has affected multitudes of people all around the world. Yet he has said that he will be a failure if his ministry is not carried on through his sons.

It is not enough for us to live faith, we must also pass it on to our children and their children. God's covenant with Abraham was with him and his seed after him. Galatians 3:29 tells us that if you and I are Christ's, then we are the seed of Abraham. It is God's intention that the same kind of enduring faith demonstrated by Abraham and Isaac and Jacob and Jesus and Peter and Paul be carried on in you and me today. He wants us to speak with the same power and authority with which they spoke. It is His intention that *all* His children live the life of faith that Jesus lived! He holds us personally responsible to see that that lifestyle of faith is passed down to those who will come after us.

In Deuteronomy 32:20 we saw that God was displeased because there was a generation of children who had no faith. God expects us to teach and train our children to have faith in Him and to look to Him as their total source of supply. In Proverbs 22:6 we are told: **Train up a child in the way he should go: and when he is old, he will not depart from it.**

Do you recall why God chose Abraham? Because He knew that he would command his children, that he would teach his children the faith life.

Can we do any less?

The Curse of Iniquity, The Blessings of Obedience

Ah sinful nation, a people laden with iniquity, a seed of evildoers, children that are corrupters: they have forsaken the Lord, they have provoked the Holy One of Israel unto anger, *they are gone away backward.*

Isaiah 1:4

In this Scripture we have seen what will happen to our children if we do not pass down to them this glorious heritage of faith: they will wind up backsliding. But look at the blessings that are promised if we do pass down that glorious faith heritage:

Isaiah 54:13 tells us: **And all thy children shall be taught of the Lord; and great shall be the peace of thy children.** *The Amplified Bible* version of the second part of this verse says **...great shall be the peace and undisturbed composure of your children.** If we pass this heritage of faith down to our children, God has promised that they will be obedient to His will, will know great peace and will enjoy a life of undisturbed composure.

In Proverbs 20:7 we read: **The just man walketh in his integrity: his children are blessed after him.** In my life and ministry I have determined that I am going to operate in excellence and without reproach. As a result, God has promised me that my children will be blessed after me. When my first grandson was born, I took him in my arms and told him: "Mark James, you are a blessed child. You picked the right family to be born into because you have a family heritage of faith. You are going to be blessed all the days of your life."

Psalm 103:17 states: **But the mercy of the Lord is from everlasting to everlasting upon them that fear**

him, and his righteousness unto children's children. Because of this promise, I expect the mercy of God to be on my children and upon my children's children.

Finally, Psalm 115:11-14 assures us:

> Ye that fear the Lord, trust in the Lord: he is their help and their shield.
>
> The Lord hath been mindful of us: he will bless us; he will bless the house of Israel; he will bless the house of Aaron.
>
> He will bless them that fear the Lord, both small and great.
>
> The Lord shall increase you more and more, you and your children.

You and I can know that our children are going to be blessed, to enjoy abundance, to be filled with faith and not fear, to live in health and not sickness and disease. Why? Because we have lived and upheld before them a lifestyle of faith. We can rejoice in the fact that if the Lord tarries they are going to receive a greater revelation of the Lord than even their parents and grandparents enjoyed because the lineage of faith has been established, and the legacy of faith has been passed down upon them.

The Household of Faith

I will sing of the mercies of the Lord for ever: with my mouth will I make known thy faithfulness to all generations.

Psalm 89:1

The Bible reveals that often it is very hard to find people who will remain faithful. Proverbs 20:6 says: **Most men will proclaim every one his own goodness: but a faithful man who can find?** People of faith, it seems, are a rare breed. That's why we must make up our minds that we are going to be among them. We must determine that for us faith is not an experiment, but a lifestyle, one that we will not only follow but pass on to our descendants, just as it was handed down to us by our ancestors.

You and I have a family heritage to recall. In Romans 4:12 the Apostle Paul says that we are to walk in the same steps of our father Abraham. And in Galatians 6:10 Paul refers to us as the household of faith.

What a title to be placed on our family crest: *The Household of Faith!*

What a heritage! What a lineage! What a legacy!

It is not uncommon for people today to hold conversations about their family, their ancestry. One of my close friends told me that someone in his family decided to trace their family tree. This person kept going back generation after generation, and the further back she went, the more disappointed she became because she discovered that the family was descended from a pirate who served under Jean Lafitte. Once that discovery was made, those people were not too thrilled about passing down their family history.

But you and I are not like that. We have a wonderful family history, one that we can be proud to pass on to future generations. It is a faith history, and it is recorded in the Bible, the Word of God.

For example, we are descended from a man called Abraham who had the audacity to believe God that he was going to be the father of nations when he knew full well that in his body he was as good as dead.

We have another ancestor named Daniel who had so much faith in his God that when he was thrown to the lions because of his faithfulness to the Lord, he was able to lie down beside the savage beasts and go to sleep in peace and security.

Another of our ancestors by the name of Elijah prophesied to the king of the land that there would be no rain for months until he had decreed an end to the drought — and it happened just as he said it would. This same man was so strong in faith and endurance that he once outran the king's horses and chariots.

We have another ancestor named Samson who was so powerful that when the Holy Ghost came upon him he could uproot city gates, slay a thousand men with the jawbone of a donkey and rip apart lions with his bare hands.

In fact, we have a whole cloud of spiritual ancestors who act as witnesses to watch over us as we live out our faith and to support us and cheer us on to ultimate victory. With that kind of family history, why should we ever be ashamed? Like Paul, we can boldly proclaim, ...**I am not ashamed of the gospel of Christ...** Why? ...**for it is the power of God unto salvation to every one that believeth....For** *therein is the righteousness of God revealed from faith to faith* [from generation to generation]: **as it is written,** *The just shall live by faith.*

You and I have a wonderful heritage and legacy of faith. And it is faith that activates God, that gives Him access to the earth, that moves His hands to intervene on behalf of those in need. God wants you and me to live by the faith of our ancestors and to pass it on to our descendants so that those who come after us will know and experience this wonderful gift — this marvelous heritage of faith.

About the Author

Dr. Jerry Savelle is a noted author, evangelist, and teacher who travels extensively throughout the United States, Canada, and overseas. He is president of Jerry Savelle Ministries, a ministry of many outreaches devoted to meeting the needs of believers all over the world.

Well-known for his balanced biblical teaching, Dr. Savelle has conducted seminars, crusades, and conventions for more than twenty years as well as holding meetings in local churches and fellowships. He is being used to help bridge the gap between the traveling ministry and the local church. In these meetings, he is able to encourage and assist pastors in perfecting the saints for the work of the ministry. He is in great demand today because of his inspiring message of victory and faith and his accurate and entertaining illustrations from the Bible. He teaches the uncompromising Word of God with a power and an authority that is exciting, but with a love that delivers the message directly to the spirit man.

When Dr. Savelle was twelve years old, God spoke to his heart as he was watching the healing ministry of Oral Roberts on television. God told him that He was calling him into the ministry. Some years later, Dr. Savelle made Jesus Christ the Lord of his life, and since that time has been moving in the light of that calling.

Dr. Savelle is the founder of Overcoming Faith Churches of Kenya, and the mission outreach of his ministry extends to more than fifty different countries around the world. His ministry also delivers the powerful message of God's Word across the United States through the JSM Prison Ministry Outreach.

Dr. Savelle has authored a number of books and has an extensive cassette teaching tape ministry. Thousands of books, tapes, and videos are distributed around the world each year through Jerry Savelle Ministries.

To contact Jerry Savelle,
write:

Jerry Savelle Ministries
P. O. Box 748
Crowley, Texas 76036

*Please include your prayer requests
and comments when you write.*

Other Books by Jerry Savelle

Turning Your Adversity Into Victory

Faith Building Daily Devotionals

The Force of Joy

*If Satan Can't Steal Your Joy,
He Can't Keep Your Goods*

Victory and Success Are Yours!

Sharing Jesus Effectively

Don't Let Go of Your Dreams

Right Mental Attitude

The Nature of Faith

God's Provision for Healing

Purged by Fire

The Established Heart

**Additional copies of this book are available
from your local bookstore.**

Harrison House
Tulsa, Oklahoma 74153

In Canada contact: Word Alive • P. O. Box 670
Niverville, Manitoba • CANADA ROA 1EO

The Harrison House Vision

Proclaiming the truth and the power
Of the Gospel of Jesus Christ
With excellence;

Challenging Christians to
Live victoriously,
Grow spiritually,
Know God intimately.